MINI-CEMENT

A Review of Indian Experience

SANJAY SINHA

INTERMEDIATE TECHNOLOGY PUBLICATIONS
1990

Intermediate Technology Publications
103/105 Southampton Row
London WC1B 4HH, UK

ISBN 1 85339 003 8

Printed in India

Preface

The subject of mini-cement has excited some debate in India in recent years. Much of it, however has been at a rather ill-informed level, relying more on impressions than concrete information. As a result, in the conduct of this study, a variety of attitudes were encountered ranging from disbelief in the capabilities of the technology on the part of the large sector, through cautious scepticism from the financial institutions, to reverential acclaim from a select few. This study represents an attempt at informed analysis in order to set the technology in its proper context in the very complex world of Indian political economy. It is hoped that it will inform, and likely that it will provoke. It is unlikely that it will dampen the debate.

The text is based on a study of the social and economic viability of mini-cement plants in the Indian economic context. It was commissioned by the Intermediate Technology Development Group (ITDG) of Rugby, U.K. as a background study to their collaboration in the research and development of the ATDA design of mini-cement plants. I would like to thank ITDG and, in particular, Frank Almond (now Chief Executive) for their sponsorship and encouragement of this work. Comments on an earlier draft were generously provided by Mel Jones of ITDG, by Frances Stewart, and by Marshall Bear and Eric Hyman of Appropriate Technology International, as well as by Frank Almond. Harro Taubmann, a West German cement technologist provided the expertise necessary to appreciate the techno-economic complexities of MCP operation.

Information for the study was obtained from sources and persons too numerous to name individually. Mention should, however, be made of the late M.K. Garg, Director (Projects) of the Appropriate Technology Development Association, Lucknow, who was one of the pioneers of mini-cement in India, and who had the dream of making cement available cheaply to the rural masses. But for his vision this study might never have been.

For extensive painstaking assistance in the conduct of this study, I would like to thank Rashmi Verma who collected, collated and tabulated a lot of the raw data, drew the figures and undertook the brunt of the proof reading of the drafts. The field survey was diligently undertaken by Kishore Kumar and Rajesh Mishra, and later assistance was provided by Upendra Mishr. I would also like to thank K.R. Saraswathy for her patient typing of sometimes confusing handwritten scripts.

Finally, and above all, my professional and personal partner, Frances, has been a constant source of inspiration, encouragement and critical appraisal. She also carried out the preliminary study of the ATDA pilot project out of which this study evolved.

None of the above is, of course, responsible for any errors of omission or commission in the study. These are entirely my own responsibility.

SANJAY SINHA

Table of Contents

Preface		*iii*
Acronyms		*vii*
Introduction		*ix*
CHAPTER 1	**CEMENT IN THE INDIAN ECONOMY**	1
	Overview	1
	The pattern of production	3
	Consumption	7
	Transport and distribution	10
	Demand	17
CHAPTER 2	**PHYSICAL FACTORS AFFECTING CEMENT OUTPUT**	20
	Limestone	21
	Coal	22
	Other raw materials	25
	Power	27
	Technical and managerial factors	28
	Environmental factors	32
CHAPTER 3	**ANATOMY OF A CRISIS**	34
	Prices and pricing policy	34
	The effects of government intervention	37
	Relative prices	39
	Alternative cementitious materials	53
CHAPTER 4	**MINI-SCALE CEMENT PRODUCTION IN INDIA**	57
	The rationale	57
	Historical development in India	58
	Technologies and designs	60
	Demand for MCPs	64
	Dissemination	67
	Government policy	68

**CHAPTER 5   MINI-CEMENT PRODUCTION: AN ECONOMIC
ANALYSIS**   70

Investment costs   70
Production costs   72
Sales realization   75
A comparison with the large-scale sector   75
Transport costs   78
The economic valuation of cement   80

CHAPTER 6   THE REALITY OF MINI-CEMENT   86

An assessment   86
Cement for the rural masses   93

**CHAPTER 7   CONCLUSIONS: SMALL VERSUS LARGE IN THE
INDIAN CEMENT INDUSTRY**   98

Resource sustainability   100
Environmental factors   100
Indigenous capabilities   102
Conclusion   103

Appendix Tables   105
Bibliography   115

Acronyms

ACC	Associated Cement Companies Limited
ATDA	Appropriate Technology Development Association
BICP	Bureau of Industrial Costs and Prices
CCI	Cement Corporation of India
CCO	Office of the Cement Controller
CEA	Central Electricity Authority
CMA	Cement Manufacturers' Association
CRI	Cement Research Institute of India, now National Council for Cement and Building Materials
DE	Development Expenditure
DGTD	Directorate General of Technical Development
DRC	Domestic Resource Cost Coefficient
ECL	Eastern Coalfields
FOR	Free on Rail
GCF	Gross Capital Formation
GDPC	Gross Domestic Profit from Construction
GNP	Gross National Product
HDPE	Heavy Density Polyethylene
HLC	High Level Committee
IDBI	Industrial Development Bank of India
IFMR	Institute of Financial Management and Research
IRR	Internal Rates of Return
ISI	Indian Standards Institution (now Bureau for India Standards)
MCP	Mini-cement Plant
MPL	Movers Private Limited
NCAER	National Council of Applied Economic Research
NCB	National Council for Cement and Building Materials
NRDC	National Research Development Corporation
OPC	Ordinary Portland Cement
ORC	Other than Rate Contract

PBFS	Portland Blast Furnace Slag Cement
PPC	Portland Pozzolana Cement
RBI	Reserve Bank of India
RC	Rate Contract
RPC	Relative Price of Cement
RRL	Regional Research Laboratory
SEB	State Electricity Board
TECS	Tata Economic Consultancy Services
VSK	Vertical Shaft Kiln
WCL	Western Coalfield
WGR	Working Group Report
WPI	Wholesale Price Index

Introduction

Cement is an essential ingredient in the process of economic development. Cement (or at least some cementitious material) is required for virtually every type of construction activity. Neither industrial nor agricultural progress is possible without it; all types of infrastructure including those of a social nature, such as health centres and schools need cement or cementitious materials. A shortage of cement can seriously affect construction programmes—as in Sri Lanka where building activity is reported to go in cycles depending on the availability of foreign exchange and in Nigeria where port congestion, particularly in the mid-1970s, brought much construction activity to a standstill while ships loaded with cement waited for a berth.

In India, the shortage of cement was for many years (but especially in the 1970s) a vital constraint on all types of development and building activity. The far-reaching consequences of this shortage are demonstrated by the fact that it was severe enough to halt the construction of a dam for several months at one stage.[a] At another it became the centrepiece of a major political scandal.[b] Though the shortages have been less acutely felt over the past three to four years, the availability and price of cement remains a major issue in the political economy of India.

[a] The Idukki dam in Kerala, Spence, 1979.
[b] A.R. Antulay, then powerfully placed as Chief Minister of Maharashtra is alleged to have mis-appropriated large sums of money as political 'donations' in exchange for preferences in the allocation of controlled price cement to private builders in Bombay at a time when the 'open market' price (in 1980-81) was more than twice the controlled price.

CHAPTER 1

Cement in the Indian Economy

Overview

The earliest use of mortar—a mixture of sand and a cementitious material to unite blocks of stone—is reported from the masonry structures of the ancient Egyptians. Burnt gypsum constituted the Egyptian prototype of cement which was also used for the aqueducts of Carthage. The use of lime, on the other hand, appears to have been discovered by the Greeks, although it was the Romans who used it as mortar mixed with sand in the modern fashion. Some evidence of the use of a cementitious material has also been found in the Indus Valley civilization of Mohenjodaro.[a]

Cement as it is known today was first produced by one James Aspdin in 1824 and was used in Europe during the last century. In India, it was manufactured for the first time near Madras in 1904, but it was not until 1914 that the first factory, established by the Indian Cement Co. Ltd. at Porbandar in Gujarat, was able to deliver packed cement on a regular basis. During the next two years two more factories were established at Katni (Madhya Pradesh) and Lakheri (Rajasthan) and the 1,000 tonnes production of 1914 expanded to 85,000 tonnes by 1918.

Table 1.1 shows the increase in factories and cement production in India on a decennial basis up to 1964 and at five-year intervals since. By 1924 six factories with a combined capacity of 559,800 tonnes had been installed, though actual production was less than half that. Production at this time far exceeded demand, particularly in the context of a prejudice against locally produced cement. The ensuing price war forced some of the companies into liquidation as some cement was sold at prices even below production cost.

[a](CMA, 1964 and Miles, 1974).

Table 1.1. Cement factories and production in India

Year	Number of factories	Production ('000 tonnes)	Annual growth rate during period
1914	1	1	—
1924	6	260	—
1934	7	950	13.8
1944	17	1,600[1]	5.3
1954	25	4,300[1]	10.4
1964	36	9,690	8.4
1969	42	13,576	7.0
1974	50	14,263	1.0
1979	56	18,238	5.1
1984	77	29,672[2]	10.2
1985/6	118[3]	33,100[4]	9.1

Sources: CMA, 1964; CCO, 1984.
[1]Estimated.
[2]Including production from mini-cement plants as reported in CCO, 1984.
[3]Including mini-cement plants (MCPs).
[4]*Financial Express* 25 March '86.

It was at this point that the first official intervention in the industry took place through a reference to the Tariff Board. In addition to recommending protection, the latter urged cooperation amongst the existing units.

The Cement Manufacturers' Association, formed in 1925, was charged with the responsibility of regulating prices. In 1927 the Concrete Association of India was formed to educate the public in the manifold uses of cement and to popularize the Indian product. Cooperation was strengthened in 1930 through the formation of the Cement Marketing Co. of India Ltd to promote and control the sale and distribution of cement at regulated prices.[a]

As a result of these efforts, the sales of cement increased considerably and by 1934 seven factories with an installed capacity of nearly 1.1 m tonnes had been established. In 1936, the process of increasing cooperation was carried to its logical conclusion with a merger of all except one of the eleven existing companies to form the Associated Cement Companies Limited.[b] The very next year,

[a]CMA, 1964 and Miles, 1974.
[a](CMA, 1964).
[b]The object of the merger was defined as...not to attain a monopolistic position (but to) make and deliver cement as cheaply as possible.

however, a rival development started with the decision of the Dalmia-Jain group to establish five new factories with a capacity of about 0.6 m tonnes. A number of other entrepreneurs entered the industry in the following years and a new price war ensued. On the eve of World War II, an agreement was reached for the Dalmia-Jain group to join the Cement Marketing Co. and the arrangement continued during the entire war period. In 1944, there were 17 factories which together produced 1.6 m tonnes of cement in that year.

Further expansion of the industry took place after the war so that, despite the loss of five factories to Pakistan in 1947, the total had risen to 25 by 1954 with a production of over 4 m tonnes. With the establishment of the Indian Standards Institution, the first Indian standards for Portland cement were laid down.

By 1964 the number of factories had risen to 36, installed capacity to 10.5 m tonnes and production had more than doubled to 9.7 m tonnes at a growth rate of 8.4 per cent p.a. White cement and Portland Blast Furnace Slag (PBFS) cement was produced in the country for the first time. A high growth rate continued until 1969, when 42 factories with an installed capacity of 14.5 m tonnes together produced 13.6 m tonnes.

After 1969 it took nearly 15 years for production to double again. Currently the cement industry, with a production of over 29 m tonnes in 1984, accounts for over 1 per cent of the GNP at factor cost and employs nearly 110,000 persons.

It is an analysis of the industry over the period since 1969 that serves as the essential background to an understanding of the scope of mini-scale cement production in India.

The pattern of production

The development of the cement industry from 1970 can be divided into three periods: 1970-1974/5, 1975/6-1978/9 and 1979/80 to date.

Between 1969/70 and 1974/5 installed capacity increased from nearly 16 m tonnes p.a. to over 20 m tonnes p.a. at an annual growth rate of 4.6 per cent (Figure 1.1). Production was virtually stagnant during this period at around 15 m tonnes p.a. Capacity utilization, below 80 per cent on average, was well below the levels prevalent in the 1960s.

During the second period, growth in installed capacity remained extremely sluggish increasing at just 3 per cent p.a., though a recovery of capacity utilization rates to around 85 per cent resulted in a faster

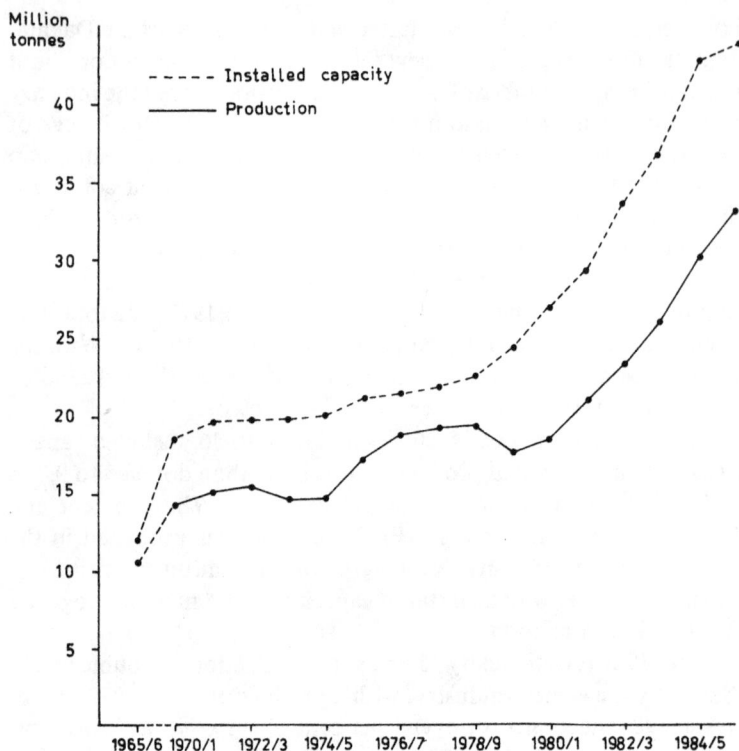

Figure 1.1 Installed capacity and production in the Indian cement industry

production growth rate of 7 per cent. In 1978/9, 22.55 m tonnes
p.a. of installed capacity produced 19.42 m tonnes of cement.

   Beginning in the year 1979/80, there was an acceleration in the
rate of increase in installed capacity, with an average growth rate
up to 1984-5 of 11.9 per cent. After a decline during the economically
disastrous year of 1979/80, production also increased at a rapid pace
(8.6 per cent p.a.) reaching an estimated level of 30 m tonnes in
1984/5. However, capacity utilization had declined again to lower
levels (around 70 per cent) than at any time since the 1930s as installed capacity accelerated to 44 m tonnes. By 1989/90, production
is expected to reach 48.66 m tonnes at a growth rate of 11 per cent
p.a.

Ownership
   Despite the post-independence tendency to favour the public sector for production in core sector industries, the figures in Table 1.2

Table 1.2. Ownership pattern of capacity and production (m. tonnes)

Sector	Capa-city (1984)	%	Produc-tion (1984)	%	New capa-city[1]	%	Total capa-city[1]	%	No of plants
Public	7.71	19	4.43	15	0.17	3	7.87	17	20
Private									
ACC	8.97	23	7.40	25	—	0	8.97	20	17
Birla									
Group	6.38	16	5.39	18	2.50	41	8.88	10	13
Others	16.19	40	11.94	40	2.99	49	19.17	42	38
Mini-cement	0.62	2	0.42	1	0.40	7	1.02	2	21
Total	39.86	100	29.58	100	6.05	100	45.91	100	109

Source: CCO, 1984.
[1]Estimated capacity in the large-scale sector up to March 1986.

show that in the case of cement the private sector has continued to dominate. The Associated Cement Companies through their 17 plants controlled 23 per cent in 1984, though this is estimated to have fallen to 20 per cent by March 1986. The public sector's share was just 19 per cent. In recent years, numerous non-traditional manufacturers such as Larsen and Toubro and Indian Rayon have entered the industry for the first time, whereas others such as the JK group and the Sahu Jains have expanded their interests substantially. The Birla group also has plans for expansion.

In 1984, production was dominated by ACC (25 per cent), followed by the Birla group (13 per cent) and the public sector.

Product type
Nine types of cement are listed by the Office of the Development Commissioner for the Cement Industry[a] as being in production in India. These are presented in Table 1.3. Over 99 per cent of the total production consists of what could be termed the 'ordinary' varieties: Ordinary Portland Cement (OPC), Portland Pozzolana Cement (PPC) and Portland Blast Furnace Slag Cement (PBFS). The relative shares of the various types of cement (Table 1.4) have shown a considerable tendency to shift in recent years; the production of PPC in particular has risen dramatically to 57.1 per cent in 1984 com-

[a]formerly known as the Office of the Cement Controller.

Table 1.3. Production of cement by type during 1984

Type	Production ('000 tonnes)
OPC	3,410
PPC	16,995[1]
PBFS	4,047
High strength OPC	65
Oil well	8
Low heat	11
Special cement:	
Railway sleeper	44
Masonry sulphate resistant	
White cement	92
Total	29,672

Source: CCO, 1984.
[1] The reported production of mini-plants has been distributed proportionately in the OPC and PPC classes.

Table 1.4. Relative share of various types of cement (per cent)

	1970	1977	1984
OPC	89.8	71.3	28.3
PPC	8.6	10.2	57.1
PBFS	9.2	17.2	13.8
White cement	0.3	0.4	0.3
Other types	0.1	0.9	0.4
Total	100.0	100.0	100.0
Production[1]	13.97	19.17	29.25

Source: CCO, various.
[1] m tonnes.

pared to just 8.6 per cent in 1970. The relative share of PBFS has also increased (though it has declined over the past two years) whereas the share of OPC has dropped sharply from nearly 90 per cent in 1970 to just 22 per cent in 1982 before rising to 28.3 per cent in 1984.

Distribution

Figure 1.2 depicts the trends in the regional distribution of installed capacity, production and capacity utilization in the Indian cement industry. It is clear from the graph that a large proportion (38 per

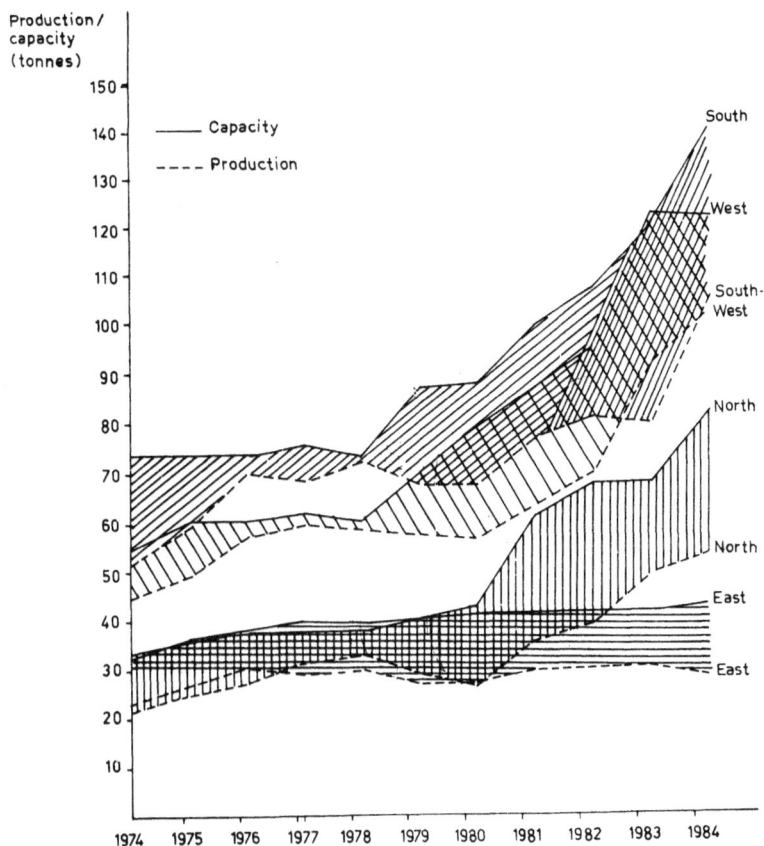

Figure 1.2 Regional distribution of production and capacity

cent) of the capacity is concentrated in the south of the country, although with more factories coming on stream in the north and west, there appears to be at least a partial tendency to equalize. The east, however, appears to be lagging in this respect. Predictably, production is also heavily concentrated in the south and west. Low levels of installed capacity in the north and east are combined with below average capacity utilization to restrict production considerably.

Consumption

During the two decades from 1963/4 to 1984/5 cement consumption in India grew from 9.33 m tonnes to 30.60 m tonnes at an

Table 1.5 Cement consumption in India (m tonnes)

Fiscal year	Production	Export	Import	Consumption[1]	% Growth[2]
1963-4	9.36	0.06	0.03	9.33	8.6
1965-6	10.58	0.04	-	10.54	6.2
1967-8	11.30	0.05	-	11.25	3.3
1969-70	13.00	0.16	-	13.54	10.1
1971-2	15.07	0.27	-	14.80	4.2
1973-4	14.66	0.20	-	14.46	(1.2)
1974-5	14.80	0.18	-	14.62	1.1
1975-6	17.29	0.54	-	16.75	14.6
1976-7	18.84	0.72	-	18.12	8.2
1977-8	19.38	0.77	0.21	18.82	3.9
1978-9	19.42	-	1.65	21.07	12.0
1979-80	17.69	-	1.80	19.49	(7.5)
1980-1	18.56	0.07	1.97	20.46	5.0
1981-2	21.06	-	1.60	22.66	10.8
1982-3	23.30	-	1.54	24.84	9.6
1983-4	27.07	neg	2.34	29.41	18.4
1984-5	30.17	0.03	0.46	30.60	4.0
1985-6	33.1[3]				

Source: CCO, various; *Cement*, 1984.
[1] Production + Import − Export.
[2] Annual basis
[3] Financial Express, 9 April, 1986.

average annual growth rate of 5.3 per cent. Since 1969/70, the average annual growth rate has been 5.5 per cent. The entire period has seen persistent shortages of cement in India and it is for this reason that Table 1.5 uses the equation:

Production + import − export = consumption

With virtually no imports until 1978/9 and only limited exports (to neighbouring countries) consumption until that time naturally followed the production pattern.[a] From 1969/70 to 1974/5 consumption was virtually static (1.4 per cent annual growth rate). With improved production (and some imports) the growth rate increased to a healthy 9.6 per cent p.a. to 1978/9. Since 1981/2 this has increased further to over 10 per cent, fueled both by better production growth rates and by the government's willingness to allow imports to ease

[a] During 1976/7 and 1977/8 exports rose to almost 4 per cent of production, roughly 75 per cent going to Iran and the UAE.

the shortages. In 1983/4 imports accounted for 8.3 per cent of domestic consumption, but fell back to 1.5 per cent in 1984/5.[a]

Per capita consumption
   The per capita consumption of cement was just 35 kg in 1983. In Table 1.6 this is compared with per capita consumption in a number of industrialized and developing countries. It is not only less than 10 per cent of the consumption in most industrialized countries, but also substantially lower than that of most developing countries. China consumes 2.7 times as much cement per capita as India and Thailand 4.2 times. Even Pakistan's consumption at 44 kg per capita was 25 per cent higher than that of India in 1983. During the 1970s (and up to 1983) the growth rate of per capita cement consumption in India was just 2.3 per cent.

Table 1.6. Per capita consumption of cement in selected countries

Industrialized countries	Per capita consumption (kg) 1983
USSR	470
Japan	678
USA	269
Italy	700
Germany (FDR)	481
France	448
Spain	816
UK	241
Developing countries	
India	35
China	93
Thailand	147
Pakistan	44
Morocco	174
Malaysia	268
Kenya	73
Sri Lanka	3
Burma	9

Source: CCO, 1984.

[a]Imports are largely from South Korea and North Korea, though miscellaneous other countries such as Taiwan, the Philippines, Romania, Poland and Japan also figure as suppliers from time to time.

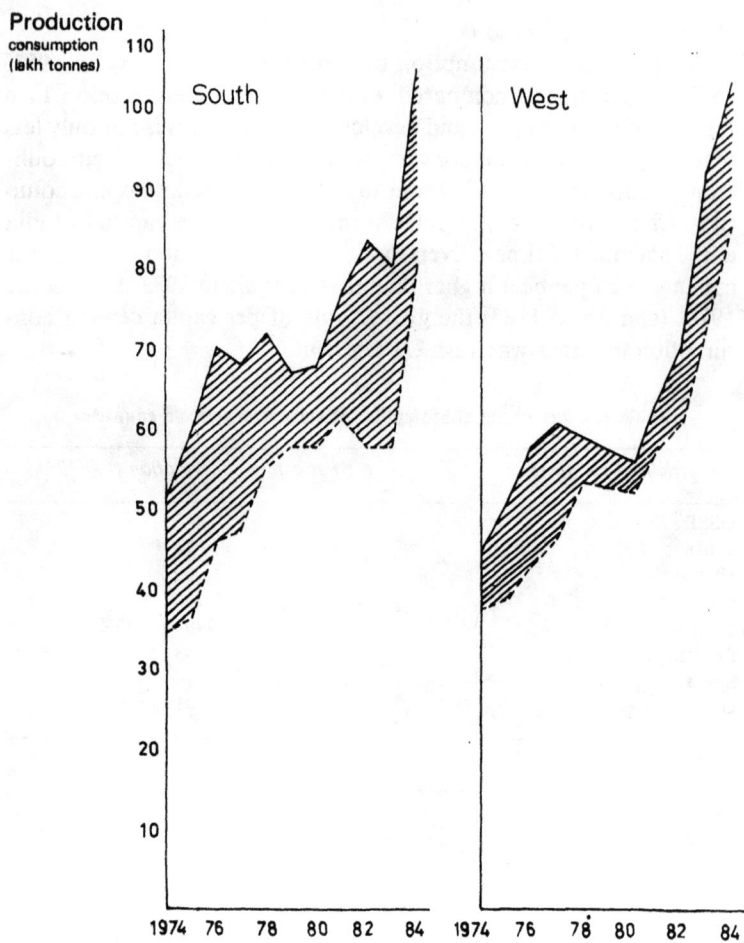

Figure 1.3   Regional imbalances in the cement industry

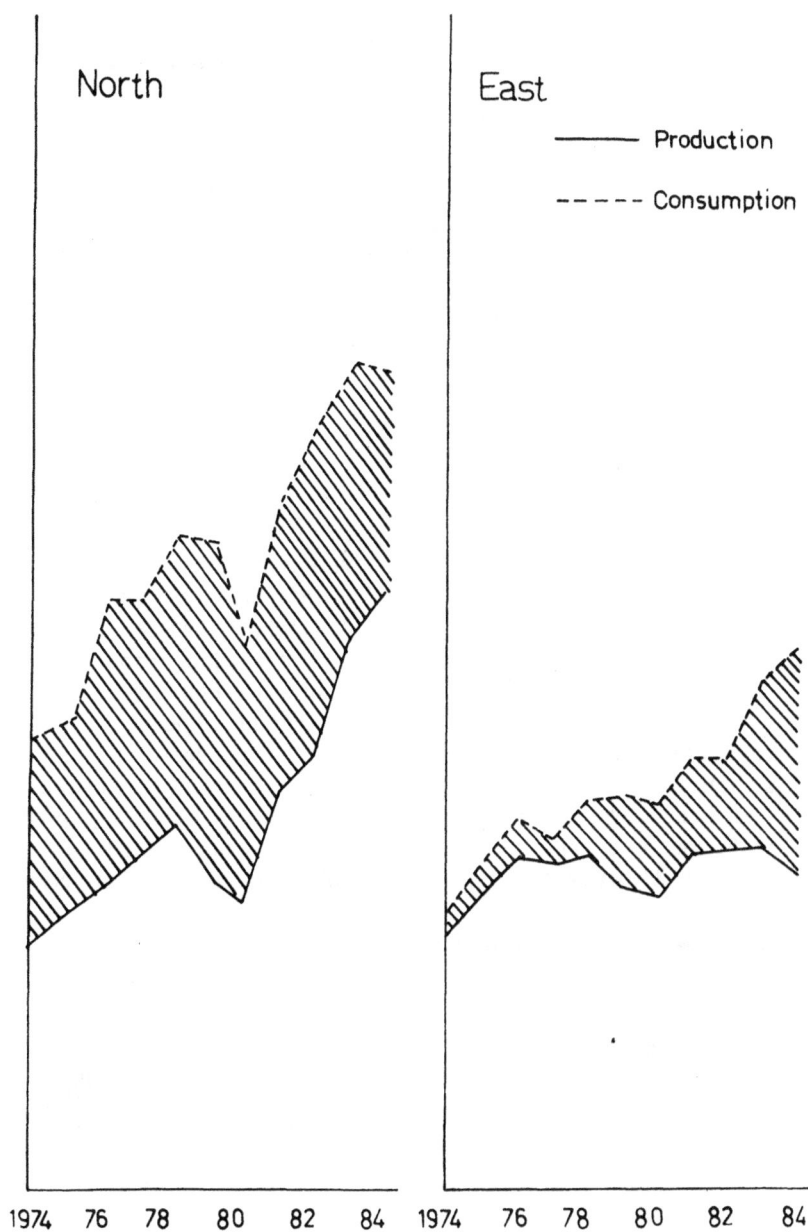

North

East

————— Production

– – – – – Consumption

1974   76   78   80   82   84   1974   76   78   80   82   84

Distribution

The implications of the regional pattern of cement production are best understood in the context of the regional consumption pattern. As depicted in Figure 1.3, consumption is fairly even over the western, northern and southern regions. A comparison with Figure 1.2 shows that while the north and east are deficit regions, the south and west produce substantial surpluses. The share of the north in both production and consumption has been static, necessitating imports equivalent to 40 per cent of production in 1984. The failure of capacity in the east to expand has resulted in a substantial deficit in that region also. The south has been exporting around 25 to 30 per cent of its production while the surplus in the west has been variable but in the 10 to 25 per cent range since 1977. Consumption growth during this period was highest in the west (8.4 per cent) and lowest in the east (2 per cent).

Transport and distribution

The regional imbalances between production and consumption evident from Figure 1.3 point to the need to transport substantial quantities of cement over long distances. Table 1.7 shows the interregional pattern in the transport of cement. Though substantial proportions stay within each region, the Table shows that the north imports nearly 35 per cent of its consumption from the west and 2.9 per cent from the south. Similarly, the east imports nearly 37 per cent of its consumption from the west. An apparent anomaly is the import by the west (which produces a surplus) of 9 per cent of its consumption from the north and 11 per cent from the south (which have deficits).[a] Other cross movements are minor in nature and largely

Table 1.7. Inter-regional transport of cement during 1984 ('000 tonnes)

From/to	North	%	South	%	East	%	West	%	Total
North	4582	61.9	—		115	2.4	756	8.9	5453
South	214	2.9	8044	98.9	196	4.1	1932	10.9	10386
East	63	0.9	9	0.1	2716	56.1	3	0.04	2791
West	2545	34.4	78	1.0	1811	37.4	5836	68.4	10270
Total	7404	100.0	8131	100.0	4838	100.0	8527	100.0	28900

Source: CCO, 1984.

[a] This can be explained in terms of transport costs (see Chapter 3).

a function of the (necessarily) arbitrary division of regions (in particular the inclusion of the central cement surplus state of Madhya Pradesh in the west). Roughly half the total cement transported is sent from the factories by rail to the distribution point and the other half by road (Table 1.8). Only very small quantities are transported along the coast by sea routes. For the relatively short distances involved from the distribution point to the retailers, road transport is used. The share of the railway in the overall transport of cement has declined from 80 per cent in the 1960s.

Table 1.8. Mode of transport[1]

Year		Rail	Quantity (m tonnes) Road	Sea	Total
1980		8.82	8.11	0.21	17.14
	(%)	51.5	47.3	1.2	100.0
1982		7.90	7.08	0.15	15.13
	(%)	52.2	46.8	1.0	100.0
1984		9.02	7.06	0.10	16.18
	(%)	55.8	43.6	0.6	100.0

Source: CCO, 1982 and 1980.

Until recently virtually all the cement available was dispatched in bags made of jute sacking. Roughly 20 per cent of cement produced is now packed in HDPE bags. Estimates available show that as much as 99 per cent of the Indian cement industry's output is transported in these bags and only 1 per cent in bulk. Only the ACC has established bulk handling facilities so far.[a] This compares with bulk supplies ranging from 30 to 90 per cent in the industrialized countries (Table 1.9). The use of jute bags results in losses through seepage from repeated handling as well as high packing costs.[b] Lined paper bags as well as the lining of jute bags is now being undertaken by some companies though this increases the cost.

[1] Figures available for the transport of levy cement only.
[a] At Okhla, near New Delhi, these facilities were established as long ago as 1960, but have not been added to since.
[b] *Reporter*, 1984 estimates losses through seepage at 4 per cent. Packing costs allowed by the government now exceed Rs 170 per tonne in an average (levy and non-levy) sales realization of around Rs 1000 per tonne.

14   MINI-CEMENT

Table 1.9. Packing of cement for transport

(per cent)

Country	In bulk	In bags
USA	90	10
Sweden	80	20
Algeria	75	25
Netherlands	73	27
Japan	70	30
Switzerland	70	30
UK	68	32
Germany (FDR)	60	40
Belgium	54	46
Denmark	54	46
Norway	49	51
France	46	54
Ireland	44	56
Morocco	43	57
Austria	39	61
Italy	34	66
Jordan	28	72
Syria	23	77
Saudi Arabia	11	89
India	1	99

Source: *Reporter*, 1984.

The distribution of cement, undertaken by the Cement Marketing Co. of India Limited since 1930, was undertaken by diverse marketing organizations after World War II. In 1956, monopoly control of distribution was handed over to the State Trading Corporation of India until 1966 when distribution controls were abolished.

In 1968 distribution controls were reintroduced under the aegis of the Office of the Cement Controller of India, Ministry of Industry. Until partial decontrol was introduced in 1982, this office regulated the distribution of cement on the basis of its quarterly assessments of likely availability and demand. Two broad quota systems were operated—central government quota and state government quota. Demand from central government departments, public sector undertakings and major industries was met from the former quota whereas demand from state departments and undertakings and small-scale industries was met from the latter. A part of the state quota was fixed for 'free sale' to the public. Generally, departmental demands were met from the Rate Contract (RC) subdivision of the quotas, whereas institutional bulk buyers were classified as 'Other than Rate Contract' (ORC) customers. RC and ORC customers were supplied cement directly under instructions from the Office of the Cement Controller (CCO). For public sale, manufacturers allotted a marketing area for the appointment of stockists/agents. However, in most cases even this category was controlled by state governments 'to eliminate hoarding, blackmarketeering and profiteering'.[a]

From 28 February 1982, this system of total distribution control was replaced by a 'dual-pricing' system which allowed genuine free sale by the factories after meeting certain obligations to supply cement to the 'levy' (or controlled price) pool. This dual pricing system is discussed in detail in Chapter 3.

Table 1 of the Appendix shows the actual consumption of cement under the various categories during the 1970-82 period. Though some private industries did obtain cement from the ORC category, the bulk of their demand was met from the public sale portion. Thus, in the Table, the sum of RC and ORC roughly constitutes public sector consumption and 'public sale' constitutes private sector consumption. As the Table shows, public sector consumption grew fairly constantly and consistently up to 1981 at a rate of growth of 10.5 per cent per annum compared to a total consumption growth rate of just 4.5 per cent. The residue available to the private sector was highly variable. Indeed, at 64.2 lakh tonnes in 1981 it was lower even than the 83.4 lakh tonnes available in 1970.

Figure 1.4 illustrates the variation of percentage share amongst the three categories and shows not only the high variability in shares but also the tendency for the private sector's share to decline and that of the public sector to rise, particularly since the late 1970s—a reflection of the acute shortages experienced during the period.[b] During this time, the absolute quantities of cement available to the public actually declined by nearly 38 per cent over a five year period. (The tendency to treat private consumption as a residue is very clear in the pre-1977 period when the public sale share rises in years of improved availability and falls in years of decline.)

---

[a]NCAER, 1979.

[b]Figures for 1982 and later years are excluded from this discussion on account of the substantive change in policy in that year.

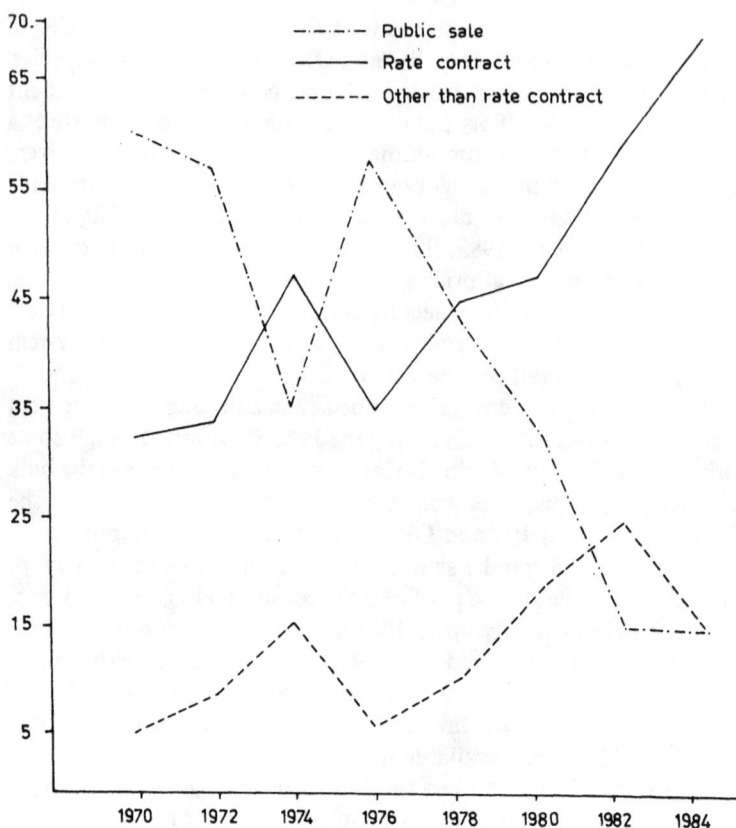

Figure 1.4 Cement despatches under various priority categories

Demand

In a historically cement-short economy where the price and distribution mechanism is grossly distorted on account of government controls, the demand for cement is difficult to measure (and obviously more difficult to predict). Nevertheless, a number of formal attempts have been made in recent years; a discussion of these can provide a means of assessing future growth in demand.

A summary of the available demand projections is provided in Table 1.10. Of the three sources, two made their estimates before 1980; their projections for 1982/3 demand are presented with ac-

Table 1.10. Projections of demand for cement

Source	Independent variable[1]	Base demand	Expected demand ED 1982/3	Implied growth rate (GR) %	ED 1989-90	GR	ED 1999-2000	GR
(Actual consumption) NCAER, 1980	VOC	consumption 1977-8	(24.84) 32.54	9.77				
World Bank 1979	GFCF	consumption 1978-9 + 5%	31.28	8.76	56.32	8.76		
		+ 10%	32.92		59.24	(12.12)[2]		
		+ 15%	34.55		62.20	(13.08)[2]		
						(14.00)[2]		
GOI, 1984	GNP	consumption 1982-3 + 20%	—	—	49.00	5.78 (9.56)[2]	87.00	5.87 (7.26)[2]
	DE							
	GCF							
	GDPC							

[1] Abbreviations—VOC: Value of Output in Construction; GNP: Gross National Product; DE: Development Expenditure; GCF: Gross Capital Formation; GFCF: Gross Fixed Capital Formation; GDPC: Gross Domestic Product in Construction.

[2] Growth rate over base year consumption.

tual consumption in that year for comparative purposes. Both these sources projected demand growth rates of around 9 per cent p.a. over base year demand using indicators for the construction sector as the independent variable. The World Bank also made allowances for shortages of 5 to 15 per cent in the base year before projecting demand. The projections in Table 1.10 suggest that the shortages in 1982/3 were in the range 20 to 28 per cent.

A more recent estimate made by the Institute of Financial Management and Research (IFMR) for the Planning Commission's Seventh Plan Working Group on the Cement Industry, assumes 1982/3 as the base year with an estimated shortfall of 20 per cent (WGR, 1984). Having rejected more direct methods (such as end-use norms) because of the 'inadequate data base' the Institute used a regression model with Gross National Product (GNP), Development Expenditure (DE), Gross Capital Formation (GCF) and Gross Domestic Product from Construction (GDPC) as the independent variables. The price elasticity of demand was not included on the assumption that the relative price of the commodity would remain constant in a controlled price regime. As Table 1.10 shows, the resulting estimates imply a growth in rate of demand under 6 per cent p.a. to the year 2000.[a]

While it is difficult to comment on the econometric validity of the IFMR model without an examination of the report, doubts certainly arise in considering the economic model on which the exercise is based.[b] In an Indian context, it could be argued that expectation of a cement shortage had become institutionalized up to 1982. Thus, planning as well as the implementation of construction projects (whether in the public or private sectors) was affected by the availability of cement, i.e. all of DE, GCF and GDPC were (and to some extent still are) affected by the supply of cement. The latter is the truly independent variable.

Similarly, in an increasingly liberal official regime with enhanced degrees of competition emerging, some decline in the prevailing relative prices of cement (RPC) has occurred over the past three years. Making an assessment, therefore, on the basis of GNP (for which higher growth rates of 5 to 7 per cent are now expected), RPC

[a]Though in terms of consumption this would imply higher growth rates if supply ultimately catches up with demand.
[b]It should be stated here that there is an *a priori* expectation of multi-collinearity between the four 'independent' variables. It is not clear whether allowance for this was made.

and the supply of cement (which has been growing at a much enhanced rate in recent years—Table 1.11), demand growth rates of the
order of 10 to 12 per cent per annum can be expected up to the year
2000.[a]

Table 1.11. Growth rates relevant to the cement industry (up to 1983/4)

(per cent)

Period (years)	Installed capacity	Production	Consumption
20	6.5	5.3	5.7
10	6.4	5.9	7.0
6	9.1	5.0	7.1
2	12.3	13.2	13.7

[a]This estimate is by way of an informed guess. It is borne out by the comments of
both producers and cement machinery manufacturers contacted by the author. It
should also be emphasised that this is a trend estimate. Temporary troughs in demand (such as that following the drought of 1987) are not ruled out.

CHAPTER 2

Physical Factors Affecting Cement Output

One of the major anomalies emerging from an analysis of the performance of the cement industry in recent years is the low capacity utilization (65 to 75 per cent), despite acute shortages in the availability of cement in the market. This phenomenon can be examined at two levels; firstly, in terms of physical factors, and secondly, in terms of policy.

For the purposes of assessment and control, the CCO requires cement factories in the large-scale sector to file detailed reports on the reasons for under-utilization of capacity. Table 2.1 indicates the importance of mechanical failure as a factor in under-utilization during the late 1970s when capacity utilization was high. By contrast, although mechanical trouble remained a significant factor in the early 1980s, it was the inadequate and erratic supply of power which emerged as the crucial factor. Power cuts and trippings accounted for around 45 per cent of the loss in 1982 and 30 per cent in 1984, while mechanical trouble was responsible for roughly 25 per cent. These figures have to be viewed with caution. For instance, in Table 2.1, while it is possible to accept that varying degrees of loss cannot be accounted for and may be due purely to inefficiencies, it is not clear why accounting in 1984 should exceed the actual loss. Also, in viewing the break down between the shortages of coal and wagons, the perennial argument between the railway companies and the coal companies about who is to blame for the shortages faced by consumers has to be borne in mind.

It is interesting to note the decline in labour troubles as a factor in production losses in the context of the increased contribution under the heading 'miscellaneous'. It can only be presumed that this is a

Table 2.1. Factors affecting capacity utilization

	1976	1980.	1984
Installed capacity (m tonnes)	21.5	25.5	39.2
Production (m tonnes)	18.7	17.9	29.2
Capacity utilization (%)	87	70	74
Under-utilization of capacity (%)	13	30	26
Factors limiting production as % of capacity			
Power cut trippings	1.91	13.05	7.77
Mechanical trouble	3.41	6.62	6.26
Teething trouble	n a[1]	1.36	5.61
Raw material shortage[2]	0.46	0.55	1.82
Shortage of wagons	0.10	1.61	0.78
Labour strike/unrest	2.66	1.10	1.42
Shortage of coal	0.02	2.98	0.07
Miscellaneous	1.62	2.41	2.31
Sub total	10.18	29.68	26.04
Not accounted for	2.82	0.32	− 0.04
	13.00	30.00	26.00

Sources: CCO, various issues.
[1]Not available separately.
[2]Including clinker shortage for grinding units.

nuance for a combination of labour inefficiencies and deliberate managerial decisions to cut production at a time when returns were low. By 1984 when large capacities were coming on stream, teething troubles had also emerged as a major factor.

In order to obtain a better understanding of the physical environment in which the cement industry operates, the availability of the major factors necessary for production is now examined.

Limestone

According to the figures of the Cement Research Institute of India, around 200,000 tonnes of limestone are contained in the earth's crust in the Indian subcontinent. Of this, nearly 60,000 tonnes constitute recoverable reserves of cement-grade material.[a] Theoretically, these

[a]ICRI, 1984. The 'Institute' has acquired enhanced grandeur and is now to be known as the National Council for Cement and Building Materials.

reserves are sufficient to produce over 45,000 tonnes of cement,or 200 years' supply even if per capita consumption builds up eventually to the levels prevailing in industrialized countries. Statewise, figures for the known reserves of cement grade limestone are contained in Table 2 of the Appendix. As the Table shows, only 10 per cent of the known deposits have been leased up to now.

In the context of the distribution of cement production in the country, Table 2.2 is illuminating. One-third of the total known reserves are concentrated in the state of Andhra Pradesh. The southern region (mainly Andhra Pradesh and Karnataka) contains over 50 per cent of the reserves. The western region (Gujarat and Madhya Pradesh) contains another 29 per cent. It is clear from these figures that cement factories have been located near the source of the main raw material. Given the bulk of the input and the consumption factor (1.2 to 1.3 tonnes of raw material are required for one tonne of cement) this is hardly surprising. However, given the regional imbalances between production and consumption, it is remarkable that 77 per cent of deposits in the north are still available while cement is transported over long distances to make up for the deficits in that region. The issue is discussed in Chapter 3.

Table 2.2. Concentration of limestone reserves

State	% of total reserves	Cumulative %
Andhra Pradesh	33.23	33.23
Karnataka	18.82	52.05
Gujarat	17.06	69.11
Madhya Pradesh	11.56	80.67
Rajasthan	4.87	85.54
Meghalaya	4.26	89.80
Himachal Pradesh	2.52	92.32
Uttar Pradesh	1.50	93.02
Maharashtra	1.42	95.24
Bihar	1.34	96.58

Source: derived from Table 2 of the Appendix.

Coal

At current levels of technology use and relative pricing structures in India, coal is the main source of fuel for firing the raw mix in cement kilns.[a] As with limestone, however, deposits of coal in the country, though substantial, are unevenly distributed. Reserves of nearly 105 bn tonnes of coal against an annual production of just 121 m tonnes in 1983—represents a very comfortable reserve position[b] (see also Table 3 of the Appendix). Again, roughly one-third of the reserves are concentrated in a single state, Bihar. While the eastern states of Bihar, West Bengal and Orissa account for nearly 70 per cent of the reserves, the cement-producing southern and western region states account for only 23 per cent and 7 per cent respectively. As a result, coal has to be transported over an average distance of 1,000 km from the coalfield to the cement plant.

Table 2.3 shows the availability position of non-coking coal (required by the cement industry) in the country. The cement industry quota is fixed on the basis of a consumption norm of 25 per cent of the installed capacity for cement production. The present annual requirement on this basis amounts to around 11 m tonnes though a production of around 30 m tonnes in 1984/5 suggests consumption of just 7.5 m tonnes. The industry's present requirements constitute around 7 per cent of overall production of non-coking coal. In quantitative terms, these are expected to rise to 25 m tonnes by the year 2000. In terms of the emergence of coal shortage as a significant factor in production loss in some years, the issue needs to be examined in more detail.

Table 2.3. Availability of non-coking coal (m tonnes)

	1980/1	1982/3	1984/5[1]
Production	82.3	93.6	111.4
Pit-head stocks	10.3	13.2	20.7
Cement industry quota	7.6	9.4	12.2
Quota as % of production	9.2	10.2	11.0
Cement industry receipts	4.8	6.1	7.6
Receipts as % of production	5.3	6.5	6.8

Sources: RBI, 1984/5 and 1982/3; WGR, 1984; and CCO 1983 and 1984.
[1] Provisional figures.

[a] Gas could emerge as a feasible alternative in the future. It is in use in some plants in industrialized countries as is fuel oil. Nevertheless, 80 per cent and more of the fuel requirement continues to be met by coal (Taubmann).
[b] *Financial Express*, 1984 (April 7).

The major sources of coal to the cement industry are listed in Table 2.4. Singareni Collieries in Andhra Pradesh are critically placed for the supply of coal to the 35 per cent of capacity located in the south. However, the historical performance of this coalfield has been poor.[a] Indeed, in 1982/3 only 55 per cent of the 'linkage' was dispatched from Singareni to the cement factories. As a result, factories in the south have to be linked both to Western Coalfields (WCL) and Eastern Coalfields (ECL), both of which involve uneconomical transport over long distances as well as increased transit losses on account of transhipments and delays. Supplies from Singareni are not only inadequate but also irregular.[b] The performance of the other coalfields was also deficient but less crucially so.

The quantity problem of coal supplies, however, is not purely that of the availability of coal but also of the loading of railway wagons. The coal industry has for many years blamed the railways for the shortage of coal to the consumer. Railway freight traffic has grown much more slowly than overall demand despite the continuing economy of rail charges relative to road transport. It is perhaps indicative of the perceived inefficiency of the railways that the rail transport coefficient for coal has fallen from over 90 per cent in the sixties to just 65 per cent in 1980/1.[c] Even in December 1984, against a daily wagon requirement of 16,000 only 13,000 wagons were being loaded though it was being hoped that with an improvement in the functioning of the railways the full requirement could be met.[d]

Table 2.4. Performance of coalfields in supplying to the cement industry 1982/3 (m tonnes)

Coalfield	Coal linkage	% of total	Dispatches	% of linkage
Singareni	2.88	31.0	1.57	55
Western	4.44	48.0	3.06	69
Eastern	0.88	9.5	0.63	71
Central	1.07	11.5	0.65	61
Total	9.28	100.0	5.91	64

Source: WGR, 1984.

[a] WGR, 1984 suggests that this is on account of poor industrial relations at Singareni.
[b] As many as 466 strikes in the collieries were reported in 1983/4 (*Financial Express,* 10 January, 1985).
[c] Ahluwalia, 1984, p 94.
[d] *Financial Express,* 20 December, 1984.

Quality

The Seventh Plan Working Group on the Cement Industry has observed that, 'Notwithstanding the frequent shortfalls in quantitative availability of coal to the industry, the quality of coal has also been deteriorating'.[a] While calorific value has fallen well below the 5,200 kcal supplied in 1978, the ash content has risen well above the 20 to 25 per cent desirable maximum. Current ash content lies in the range 30 to 35 per cent though coal with up to 50 per cent ash and heating value of 3,000 kcal has also been reported.[b] The consequence of this quality deterioration is not only the increase in the specific consumption of coal but also an increase in the handling needs (increasing pressure on the transport system) and reduction in grinding capacity. Furthermore, quality variations cause heat loads to vary, affecting processing and reducing the life of the kiln lining. The working group has suggested more selective mining as well as pithead beneficiation amongst other measures to deal with this problem.

Other raw materials

Clay and other additives

Clay is often required as an additive to the raw mix (when calcium content of limestone is high) to give the right proportion of silica. The use of clay varies from zero to 25 per cent.[c] This is, generally, easily available near cement plants, except in the case of some plants in Karnataka, Gujarat and Meghalaya which have to transport it from a distance. High alumina bauxite and high quality iron are also sometimes required. Plants in Rajasthan in particular are located at some distance from the source of these materials and have to pay high transport costs.[d]

Gypsum

Gypsum is added to clinker at the grinding stage to improve the setting qualities of finished cement. The quantity used can vary from 4 to 7 per cent according to the quality of clinker as well as that

[a] WGR, 1984, p 76.

[b] As a result, some cement manufacturers are starting to think in terms of setting up washeries (*Financial Express,* 31 October, 1984).

[c] NCAER, 1979.

[d] WGR, 1984.

of gypsum but is generally around 5 per cent. The sources of supply of the material are extremely limited, being confined to Rajasthan and Tamil Nadu. Available figures show total reserves of the order of 1,200 m tonnes, of which nearly 89 per cent are located in Rajasthan and 9 per cent in Jammu and Kashmir (though the latter do not appear to have been exploited to any significant extent).[a] The 16 m tonnes of reserves in Tamil Nadu on the other hand have been exploited extensively for the industry in the south. Recent discoveries in Eastern Bhutan are likely to lower the cost incurred by plants in the eastern region.[b] The requirements of the industry are around 1.5 m tonnes at present and likely to rise to 4 m tonnes by the year 2000.

Industrial wastes

Substantial quantities of fly ash (about 14 m tonnes) used for the production of PPC are currently produced as waste by the thermal power plants around the country. Though the IS specifications allow for the use of up to 25 per cent fly ash for PPC, the working group has calculated that no more than 10 per cent can in fact be utilized, given the quality of clinker being produced by the industry at present.

Granulated blast furnace slag, a by-product of steel plants, can also be used as an additive to gypsum and clinker at the grinding stage to produce PBFS. Substantial proportions of slag can be added (particularly if the lime content is high) producing 1.4 to 1.5 tonnes of PBFS with one tonne of clinker. Slag use, according to IS specifications, can be 25 to 65 per cent, resulting, with the addition of extra gypsum and fine grinding, in a product with similar strength to OPC but higher resistance to sulphates, water and high temperatures and lower heat of hydration. The setting and curing time also exceeds that of OPC. It is particularly suitable for use in sea water, sulphate-bearing water and alkali soils as well as for general purpose construction.

The production of PBFS is, at present, limited by the production of just 1.8 m tonnes of granulated slag by the steel industry.

The use of industrial wastes in cement production can reduce the capital costs of cement production (by as much as 35 to 40 per cent in the case of PBFS), enhance cement availability and open up the possibility of cost reductions by the location of grinding units near

[a]NCAER, 1979 and Table 4.2.
[b]WGR, 1984.

power and steel plants in the high consumption areas. The easy availability of fly ash has clearly been one important factor in the increasing share of PPC in the product mix of the industry, whereas the growth of PBFS production has been constrained by the limited availability of granulated slag.

Power

The cement industry's share of total electricity consumption by industry is around 5 per cent. At an average consumption rate of 125 kWh per tonne of cement it should show an increase from 2,400 GWh in 1977/8 to 3,300 GWh in 1983/4. As a share of overall electricity consumed, that of the cement industry had declined from 2.8 per cent in 1974/5 to 2.3 per cent in 1981/2.

The importance of power cuts and trippings as a factor responsible for loss of production in the cement industry is clear from Table 2.1. The shortage of power is a chronic problem affecting the entire Indian economy. According to estimates of the Central Electricity Authority, shortages over the period 1974/5 to 1982/3 ranged from 5.8 per cent up to 16.1 per cent (Table 4 of the Appendix). In 1982/3 it was 9.2 per cent.[a] The problem of power shortage faced by all Indian consumers is accentuated in the case of the cement industry. A large proportion (68 per cent) of cement capacity is located in the states of Tamil Nadu, Meghalaya, Andhra Pradesh, Rajasthan and Karnataka; except Andhra Pradesh these are all power-deficit states. Table 2.5 shows the loss of production on account of power cuts in some of the major cement-producing states. In addition to power cuts notified by the electricity authorities, there are often unscheduled interruptions and fluctuations in voltage.

At the same time, cement manufacture is a continuous process and a sustained supply of power is essential. Even a small interruption can result in a disproportionate production loss. The working group on the cement industry has calculated that for the purpose of daily rostering it would be necessary to make 25 per cent power available to wet process and 40 per cent to dry process plants even at times of high cuts in supply to maintain production.[b]

---

[a]Estimates presented in Ahluwalia, 1984. She points out that these shortages may be underestimated on account of the restricted base year consumption used by the CEA to estimate requirement. The problem is similar to that in estimating demand for cement.

[b]WGR, 1984, p 44.

Table 2.5. Loss of production on account of power cuts 1984

States	Quantity ('000 tonnes)	As a % of total under-utilized capacity	% loss of installed capacity
Rajasthan	400	58.6	9.6
Uttar Pradesh	374	22.2	14.5
Andhra Pradesh	435	30.9	7.9
Tamil Nadu	48	16.6	1.1
Karnataka	765	49.1	19.7
Bihar	319	26.1	12.5
Gujarat	73	9.5	2.6
Maharashtra	36	5.2	0.3
Madhya Pradesh	430	91.3	5.9

Source: CCO, 1984.

For this reason and because the supply position is not expected to improve during the Seventh Plan Period (1985/90), the cement industry has been advised to install standby generators to meet 40 per cent of its requirements during periods of power loss. Though some have already done so and others are in the process, the use of 'captive' power increases production costs substantially because the capital cost of the plant is increased and the generating cost is substantially higher than the price of grid supply.[a] The use of diesel for operating the sets also increases the overall burden on the economy. Some units (13 in 1982) have established thermal power plants for their own use but this increases their coal 'linkage' with all the attendant problems of supply. It alleviates but does not necessarily resolve the power crisis.

Technical and managerial factors

Technology

The evolution of technology for the large-scale manufacture of cement has seen the emergence of a 'wet' process, followed by variations on 'semi-dry' and 'dry' processes. The most favoured technology at present is the dry process with precalcinator. In enabling up to 95 per cent of the calcination to take place in a chamber

[a]By March 1984, 224 MW of captive generation capacity had been installed and another 224 MW was in the process of installation.

or duct outside the rotary kiln, the precalcinator improves the energy efficiency of the process, at the same time increasing the throughput (capacity) of the kiln. Table 5 of the Appendix lists the major variations in basic parameters across the technologies. The figures suggest a 45 per cent reduction in energy consumption in the kiln and a 250 to 300 per cent increase in output, offset by an 8 per cent increase in power requirements in converting from a wet to a dry process kiln. The conversion cost of Rs 1,150-1,250 per tonne compares with a new investment cost of Rs 1,300-1,700 per tonne.[a]

Of the 72 large cement plants in the country in 1983, 33 employed the wet process technology, seven the semi-dry process and 37 the dry process.[b] This technological distribution is constantly changing, however, as plants are being modernized and converted to dry process and new plants based on the dry process are coming on stream. The WGR, 1984 shows that 63 plants had plans for modernization in 1983. The working group estimated that as much as 3 m tonnes of capacity would need to be scrapped every five years—a total of 12 m tonnes by the year 2000—because plants had exceeded their useful life (35 years).

In terms of kilns, more recent information shows that over 60 per cent of those in the large-scale sector still use the conventional wet process. On account of their low productivity, these provide just one third of capacity which is dominated by the modern, high productivity, dry process technology (Table 2.6).

Table 2.6. Process technologies in the large-scale sector[1]

Process	Kilns (No)	% of kilns	% of capacity
Wet	93	60.8	33.2
Semi-dry	7	4.6	3.0
Dry	63	34.6	63.8
Total	163	100.0	100.0

[1]Latest available information presented in *Financial Express*, 26 March, 1986.

[a]WGR, 1984 and Palkhiwala, 1983. More recent information from modern large scale plants shows that current (1985/6) investment costs lie in the range Rs. 1,000 – 1,100.
[b]WGR, 1984, p 87—some used a combination of technologies.

Information available on the size distribution of cement plants is presented in Table 2.7.[a] This shows clearly the trend towards the establishment of larger size plants in the Indian industry. Indeed, the average installed capacities of new units coming on stream suggest a distinct cut off in the mid-1970s when the switch from wet to dry process was accompanied by (and probably affected by) a preference for larger scale plants. Thus the minimum economic scale (m.e.s.) of 600 tonnes per day in the early 1970s increased to 1,200 t.p.d. in the late 1970s. The advent of precalcination has pushed the m.e.s. even higher to 2,000 tonnes per day.[b] These trends in the Indian industry are roughly in line with developments internationally though with a time-lag of about five years.

Table 2.7. Size distribution of cement plants

Capacity (tonnes)	No (1976)	No (1984)
Less than 2.0	8	9
2.0 – 4.0	22	28
4.0 – 6.0	17	21
6.0 – 8.0	4	6
8.0 – 10.0	2	5
10.0 and above	2	6
Total	55	75

Sources: (1976 figures) NCAER, 1979; CCO, 1984.

Machinery manufacture

Given that all the raw materials for cement manufacture are available locally, it is to the credit of the cement machinery manufacturers in India that the industry is largely an indigenous one. In 1978, plants up to 1,200 tonnes per day capacity had an import content of less than 5 per cent. However, the industry stagnated up to this time due to the slow growth of the cement industry. As demand picked up in the late seventies, new collaboration agreements brought a fresh flow of technology so that today the industry is capable of

[a] The manner of presentation of some of the statistics is so ambiguous as to suggest that up-dated figures were not in fact available at the time of compilation of these documents.
[b] Although this does not necessarily mean a larger physical size of kiln as precalination enables a higher throughput as explained earlier.

delivering up to 18 plants per annum in the 600-3,000 tonnes per day range. As many as 10 to 12 plants with the latest precalcination technology were under manufacture in 1983. The import content of these plants is 20 to 25 per cent at present but is expected to fall to around 10 per cent in the next two years.[a] There are few complaints about the quality of these plants, though delays in delivery schedules are common. It is also worth noting here that a study of the machine manufacturing sector in India by the World Bank found the cement machinery industry to be economically efficient despite higher protection on inputs than on outputs.[b]

Though the Indian cement industry appears to be well served in the availability of the latest machinery to a good standard of quality at relatively low prices, it is hampered (as the earlier discussions show) by problems in the quantitative and qualitative availability of inputs, particularly coal and power. This has affected capacity utilization. At the same time, the significance of the residuals in Table 2.1, as well as that of mechanical trouble in production loss, suggests that other factors may also be at work. Frequent mechanical trouble, for instance, is a clear indication of poor maintenance.

Linked to maintenance is the dust problem endemic in cement manufacture. This not only has a damaging affect on the environment and health of workers and neighbours, it also affects the life and maintenance needs of machinery. Although detailed norms for the industry have been established, they are not being rigorously enforced at present—even units with installed electrostatic precipitators are often found not to be using them.[c]

These indications of managerial deficiencies are further strengthened by some other well-known features of the Indian cement industry:

- the mining of limestone is not sufficiently selective to ensure consistent quality limestone
- despite the variable quality of coal, a uniform coal feed (and hence consistent quality clinker) is not always ensured through proper blending
- instrumentation is often inadequate and instruments are poorly maintained

[a]WGR, 1984, p 67.
[b]EPW, October 12 1985.
[c]The need for eifective pollution control has also been emphasized by the working group.

- the productivity of labour is low. (Production per capita in 1982 was only 280 tonnes compared to 2,376 tonnes in West Germany.[a] While the figures are not strictly comparable, given the Indian socio-political situation, they are so far below international standards as to raise serious doubts about the competitiveness of the industry in any long-term requirement for supply to exceed demand. It is also well below the traditional norm of one worker per tonne of daily production or 330 tonnes per capita per annum.)

Whilst the fourth of these features may not, strictly, be the result of managerial deficiencies, the first three clearly are. However, the question of whether these deficiencies arise as the result of a lack of skills or motivation is a moot point. The extent of efficiency in an industry characterized by a supply constraint and either policy imposed stagnation or (more recently) monopoly profits, is bound to be limited. It is perhaps indicative of the industry's attitude in recent years that the ISI has had to suspend licences for several cement producers for not adhering to quality standards.[b]

Environmental factors

As indicated in the previous section, although there are detailed pollution control norms for the cement industry, not much attention is currently being paid to their implementation. There is a general feeling in the industry that the blanket restriction on emission at 250 mg/NM³ is very difficult to achieve. The problem is complicated in India not only by the obsolescent nature of the technology in use but also by disturbances in production from power interruptions and the poor quality of coal. The industry does not accept that the installation of sophisticated pollution control equipment for arresting chimney dust would reduce cost and enable savings by utilizing materials which would otherwise have escaped. An exponential cost/benefit equation makes this argument irrelevant from the industry's point of view.[c] The government, perhaps concerned about already high investment and production costs, has done little to enforce the pollution control norms.[d]

---

[a]CCO, 1982 and Taubmann, 1985.
[b]*Financial Express*, 1 January 1986.
[c]*Cement*, July-September 1983.
[d]Though some companies like ACC have voluntarily attempted to conform to them as part of their 'social obligation'.

An apparently more pressing environmental issue which has excited some concern in recent years is the depredation of the landscape caused by limestone quarries. This has been particularly controversial in the case of the scenically beautiful Dehra Dun valley and Mussoorie hills of Uttar Pradesh where the indiscriminate quarrying of high quality limestone has led to the appearance of ugly gashes in the countryside and caused erosion, landslides and an increase in dust levels. A refusal to extend mining leases here has led to protracted legal battles, surreptitious mining and consequent allegations of corruption in high places.[a] The issue has alerted environmentalists to the potentially harmful effects of cement plant location and could become an important consideration in the future choice of plant sites.

[a] *Business India,* 24 October, 1983, *Times of India,* 15 October, 1983.

CHAPTER 3

Anatomy of a Crisis

In its initial decades, the Indian cement industry was characterized by problems of oversupply and price wars amongst the manufacturers competing for limited markets. In recent years, the situation has been reversed—demand has expanded considerably, supply has stagnated and prices have been strictly regulated on the one hand and surged on the open (usually black) markets on the other. The industry has now emerged from a crisis situation but the consumer (particularly the rural consumer) is still plagued by high prices and, to a lesser extent, by a problem of access.

This chapter analyses the development of the present situation—government policy and its effects on the prices and availability of cement, the resulting investment patterns in the industry and the contributing effect of public perceptions to overall demand patterns.

Prices and pricing policy

Price controls have been applied to the cement industry almost continuously since 1942. The major components of the controlled price have consisted of an ex-factory price (retention price), packing charges (for bagged cement) allowed separately, excise duties and a uniform freight charge applicable all over the country. The sum of these yields is the FOR (i.e., the supplier pays freight charges until the goods reach the railway station) price of bagged cement to which incidental charges[a] and sales tax are added at the state level. The basis for fixing retention price has varied over the years. In the initial stages (1942-46), cost-plus pricing for individual plants was used. Between 1946 and 1952 the principle of 'lead price' was employed based on the production costs of ACC, the dominant producer at the time.

[a]Handling, local transport and godown charges as well as retailer's margin.

In 1952 it was decided that the industry should be 'subjected to periodical reviews by expert bodies with a view to determining reasonable prices to producers as well as to consumers and also to determine a proper distribution policy to ensure cement availability in all parts of the country'. A series of studies of the industry were conducted by a Tariff Commission over the next 20 years.

Despite these studies, however, the prices allowed to the industry by the government were usually at variance with the recommendations of the Tariff Commission. A major part of the responsibility for the crisis in the industry is attributable to apparently political decisions to ignore the recommendations of official expert committees. While the first report in 1953 recommended a base of Rs 72 per tonne FOR, the government fixed a price of Rs 67 per tonne with an additional 7.5 to 18 per cent for high cost units. In 1961, the Tariff Commission recommended ten separate retention prices and a provision for price escalation to compensate for any rise in the price of coal and fuel. Instead, the government fixed a uniform price allowing differentials for three high-cost producers only.

After the decontrol of 1966/7 a uniform retention price based on weighted average production cost of all operating plants and a target return of 14 per cent on capital employed[a] was fixed in 1968. In 1969, an ad hoc price increase was granted to the industry but this was not thought to be adequate[b] and after a fresh study by the Tariff Commission a uniform retention price of Rs 100 per tonne was fixed. This continued unchanged until September 1973 when an ad hoc increase of Rs 10 was granted.

The 1974 Tariff Commission report, based on the cost data of 23 units, recommended a substantial increase of 27 per cent in the retention price. The device of splitting cost components into escalatory and non-escalatory items was also used, the escalatory items being wages and daily allowance price and freight of coal, power tariff and freight of limestone.

Although the Commission recommended an automatic increase when costs increased by Rs 0.50 per tonne, the government restricted the frequency of escalations to once a year. The industry at this time was continually dissatisfied even with the basis for allowing a return and accordingly, although retention prices increased to around Rs

[a]Profit before deduction of tax and interest as a percentage of share capital, reserves and surplus and long term borrowings.
[b]NCAER, 1978.

160 per tonne by 1976/7 (Table 6 of the Appendix), very little new
investment took place. At this time, the Bureau of Industrial Costs
and Prices (BICP) estimated that in fact a 14 per cent return on
capital employed amounted to no more than a 5 per cent tax return
on equity (given a debt-equity ratio of 2:1). The BICP recommended a post tax return of 12 per cent on net worth.

The BICP formula accepted by the government in September 1977
was made applicable to all new and substantially expanded units.
A retention price of Rs 296 per tonne was announced for such units
which started commercial operation from or after April 1977. At
the same time, a High Level Committee (HLC) carried out a further study of the price structure and, on the basis of data from 19
plants, recommended a three-tier pricing system for old plants.

This differential pricing system with annual escalations was continued until February 1982 when, in a revolutionary move, partial
decontrol was introduced. Under the new scheme, all units were required to supply cement equivalent to a certain proportion of installed capacity at levy (or controlled) rates while production above
this level could be sold in the open market. The new policy
distinguished between old and profit-making large-scale plants on
the one hand and new and 'sick' (chronically unprofitable) units on
the other. Table 3.1 shows the extent of the levy quotas imposed

Table 3.1. Levy quota imposed on the cement industry

Effective date	March 1982 to July 1984	July 1984[1]	July 1985[2]	March 1986[3]
Large Scale:				
Units in production before January 1982	66.6	65.0	60.0	60.0 45.0[4]
New units in production after January 1982	50.0	45.0	40.0	40.0 30.0[4]
'Sick' units	50.0	45.0	40.0	40.0
Mini-plants:	Nil	Nil	Nil	Nil

Sources: WGR, 1984; *Financial Express,* 19 July 1984 and 5 June 1985.
[1] Per cent of installed capacity.
[2] Per cent of actual production.
[3] *Financial Express,* 22 March 1986.
[4] In response to the CMA's plea for reducing the levy obligation for that part of their
production which results from a licensed capacity utilization beyond 80 per cent, the
government has agreed to this relief linked to capacity use beyond 100 per cent.

by the new policy. The proportions were reduced in July 1984. In June 1985 the control was relaxed further by reducing the proportions to 60 per cent for old units and 40 per cent for new and sick units. The basis for calculation was changed from installed capacity to actual production.

Simultaneously with the introduction of dual pricing, a uniform retention price of levy cement was introduced while the Cement Manufacturers Association announced voluntary price restraint on open market sales. For the first time, separate retention prices for OPC and PPC were announced at Rs 335 and Rs 320 per tonne. These prices, however, were substantially lower than the Rs 385 and Rs 370 per tonne recommended by the Ghosh Committee.[a] On the open market, prices were originally fixed at Rs 65 per bag (Rs 1,300 per tonne) by the CMA but in most states these did not hold. Open market prices settled between Rs. 1,100 and Rs 1,200 per tonne corresponding to an average FOR price of Rs 1,005 per tonne and an ex-works realization of Rs 705 per tonne. In 1985, these prices become highly volatile ranging from Rs 1,200-1,600 per tonne. Assuming an average realization of Rs 1,340 per tonne, at present, this corresponds to an FOR price of Rs 1,270 per tonne and an ex-works realization of around Rs 800.[b]

The effects of government intervention

As the foregoing discussion shows, the intervention of the government in the cement industry has, over the years, been largely of a

[a] *Business India*, 1982. The Committee had also recommended that 25% of the capacity of old units and 40% of new units be freed for open market sale. The Committee was appointed by the Government to recommend a strategy for the development of the cement industry.

[b] This is calculated in the following way:

		Rs/tonne
Market price		1,340
Margin to stockist and expenses		70
Sales Tax		80
FOR price		1,190
Excise	225	
Packing	100	
Cement Regulation Account	10	
Freight	105	440
		750

The freight charge assumes an average distance for non-levy cement transport of 400-500 km—less than the 800 km for levy cement.

discretionary nature. Both price and distribution controls were ostensibly for the purpose of ensuring the availability of an essential commodity for development projects as well as for private housing. In fact, the late 1960s and 1970s, the period of the most rigid controls, saw the severest shortages of the commodity and in the latter years the fastest increases in prices.

These shortages were felt more acutely in some parts of the country than in others.[a] An examination of the effects of price and distribution controls shows that these distortions arose from the very nature of the discretionary controls imposed rather than from any problems inherent to the industry.

In the early years, the use of cost plus as a basis for price fixing discouraged efficiency as prices would be adjusted downwards if costs were reduced. In later years the system of uniform prices ignored the relative cost differences between plants. Combined with the policy of freight equalization this meant that locational optimization did not take place. Location near the sources of limestone took precedence over location near markets. This is partly responsible for the regional imbalances in production relative to consumption shown in Chapter 1.

The theoretical basis for a uniform price policy is the apparent penalty it imposes on inefficiently managed units relative to the profits it makes available to efficiently managed units of the same technological genre. It assumes that all units have a similar cost structure and ignores any differences in production costs arising from locational factors, such as the quality (and beneficiation needs) of locally available limestone, varying degrees of difficulty in quarrying limestone and the rate at which coal and power are available. Perhaps most importantly, it ignores the manufacturing technology employed by the plant and its age. The effect of this is to penalize new investment (undertaken at a higher unit capital cost for reasons of inflation) neutralizing in the short term any production economies made available by technical change. In order to encourage new investments, price increases have to be sufficiently frequent to allow for the constantly increasing capital charge.

The introduction of a differential price for new and substantial expansions in 1977 and of a three-tier pricing system in 1979 went some way to reducing these anomalies. By allowing a portion of each

---

[a] Large cities with acute housing shortages, such as Bombay and Calcutta, were the most severely affected.

plant's production to be sold on the open market the system of partial decontrol enables cement producers to increase substantially their average realization.

In the context of the objectives of government policy, the net effects of price control can be assessed from trends in the relative price of cement and from the changing profitability position of the companies:

Relative prices
Table 3.2 shows the variation in the price obtained for cement by producers on the one hand and that paid by consumers on the other. The index of retention prices is deflated by the wholesale price index of all commodities to obtain the relative variation in revenues allowed to producers. For relative consumer price, it is the FOR price relative to consumers' purchasing power that is relevant. Since a substantial proportion of private cement consumption is attributable to those engaged in the organized sector, the available series on public sector salaries is used as an indicator of purchasing power.

It is clear from the Table that price increases allowed to producers were much lower than the general level of inflation between 1965/6 and 1973/4. Increases granted after that did not compensate fully for inflation until 1978/9 (for old units) and 1977/8 (for new units). Subsequently, there were further erosions in the unit revenue as the intermittent price increases compensated for inflation to varying degrees. It is interesting to note that despite the persistent shortages of the past decades, the real value obtained by producers was never allowed to rise significantly above that prevailing in 1965/6 and was substantially below it over virtually the entire period. Even the differential allowed to new units was allowed to erode until the introduction of dual pricing. Since then, realizations on open market sales have been at roughly twice the level of retention prices.

At the same time, relative prices paid by consumers remained more or less in concert with consumers' measured purchasing power. Despite the shortage, there was no tendency for relative prices to increase in the officially regulated market. On the illegal open market in the early 1980s, prices ranged from Rs 2,000-3,000 per tonne,[a] three to four times the regulated price. The introduction of dual pric-

[a] *Business India*, various (Commodities Section).

Table 3.2. Relative price variation of cement (1970/1 = 100)

Year	Retention price	Retention price (new units)[4]	FOR price	WPI all commodities	Relative price of cement to producers[1]	Relative price of cement to producers (new units)[4]	Index of earnings[2]	Relative price to consumers[3]
1965/6	81			72	113			
1970/1	100		100	100	100		100	100
1971/2	101		104	108	93		108	96
1972/3	101		108	121	83		106	102
1973/4	112		113	158	71		102	111
1974/5	155		159	174	89		135	118
1975/6	154		169	163	94		164	103
1976/7	153		171	182	84		163	105
1977/8	170	285⁴	172	183	93	156⁴	184	93
1978/9	227	285	207	191	119	149	205	101
1979/80	249	285	228	232	107	123	228	100
1980/1	243	298	230	271	90	110	260	88
1981/2	313	332	272	277	113	120	295	92
1982/3	339	679	332	295	115	230	329	101
1983/4	335	707	392	322	104	220	396	99
1984/5	374	707	436	338	111	210	429	106
1985/6	374	810	455	358⁵	104	226	n.a.	—

Sources: Cement Price Index derived from Table 5 of the Appendix; index of earnings from Economic Survey, GOI.

[1] $\dfrac{\text{Retention price}}{\text{WPI all commodities}} \times 100$

[2] Index of per capita earnings of public sector employees.

[3] $\dfrac{\text{FOR price}}{\text{Index of earnings}} \times 100$

[4] Index of retention price allowed to new units, index of non-levy realization from 1982/3.

[5] As on 31 December 1985.

ing in 1982 and the consequent legislation of the open market saw an immediate drop in prices to Rs 1,100-1,200 per tonne, around twice the levy price at the time. Currently, with the market price of levy cement climbing to over Rs 1,000 per tonne, the open market premium averages just 35 per cent.

The graphical comparison of relative prices (Figure 3.1) shows the wide gap between producer and consumer prices until the increasing realism in government policy, beginning in 1977. Much of this difference was on account of the recovery of increased taxes from the cement industry. In recent years, this gap has been much narrower, but the industry has increasingly been used as a means of resource mobilization. As a proportion of ex-factory retention price, excise duties on cement increased from 31 per cent in 1970/1 to 52 per cent in 1975/6. By 1981/2 these had fallen to 22 per cent but have increased continuously since then reaching the level of 58 per

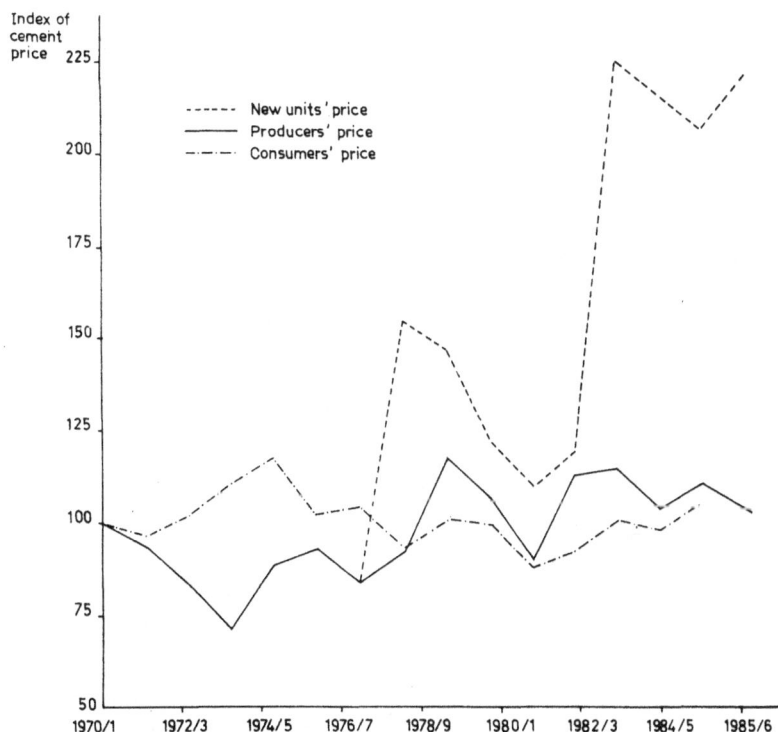

Figure 3.1 Relative price variation of cement (1970/7 = 100)

cent in March 1985 (See Table 5 of the Appendix). In recent years, freight and packing charges have also tended to escalate substantially. Packing charges in particular have increased from just Rs 64 per tonne (20 per cent of retention price) in 1981/2 to Rs 177 per tonne (46 per cent) in March 1985.[a]

It is interesting to note that, as a proportion of total excise revenue, revenues from cement accounted for 2.0 to 3.3 per cent between 1966/7 and 1981/2. In three years after that, this proportion rose to as much as an estimated 5.8 per cent in 1984/5 (Table 7 of the Appendix).[b]

Profitability

An idea of the extent of interplant variation in the cost of cement production in Indian conditions is provided by the information in Tables 3.3 and 3.4. These show total production costs in 1982/3 varying by 30 per cent around the average, though differences for individual cost items are much higher. The lack of systematic interregional variation in these costs suggests that differences are highly localized in terms of economic as well as technological and managerial factors. In some cases, differences in the proportion of various types of cement produced (OPC, PBFS and PPC) would be responsible for this variation.

Although the system of dual pricing is also based essentially on uniform retention prices, the freeing of a proportion for open market sale based on the age and to some extent the earning capacity of the old units has enabled the industry to improve its profitability. Figures available for 1982/3 show that for 47 units an average net loss of Rs 36 per tonne on levy sales was converted into an overall

[a] This is largely on account of the continuing use of jute bags for packing cement. In order to minimize seepage and transportation losses the government insists upon the use of new bags for this purpose. *Reporter,* 1984 has calculated that for the 1984/5 cement output of around 32 m tonnes, the industry would require 3.5 lakh tonnes of jute goods (or about 30 per cent of the average annual output of the jute industry) for packing. Given a declining trend in jute production and a fast growing trend in cement production, it is not surprising that packing charges are increasing at this rate. With an improved jute crop and some shift to synthetic bags, packing charges were reduced in 1985/6.

[b] It may be of some significance that, despite the improved overall price realization made possible by dual pricing since 1982/3, capacity utilization has not shown a tendency to improve to the levels of the mid-1970s. This could be related to the dramatic increase in excise duties in recent years and points to the possibility of some degree of under-reporting of production.

Table 3.3. Variation of costs of ordinary Portland cement production in the large scale sector (1982/3) (Range in Rs per tonne)

	North	South	East	West	India[1] (average)
Raw materials	51-116	39-107	406	33-67	
Power	52-86	22-78 ⎫		29-100	
Coal	70-139	51-106 ⎭		47-132	
			31		
Labour	25-96	5-54	0-5	16-49	
Other	64-196	82-170	16	17-126	
Total	351-483	310-575	453	344-485	426

Source: TECS, 1984.
[1] Average costs are not available for each item.

Table 3.4. Distribution of OPC producing units by cost of production (1982/3)

Range (Rs)	North	East	South	West	Total
300-339	-	-	2	-	2
340-400	2	-	3	5	10
401-450	-	1	3	-	4
451-500	3	-	5	2	10
501-550	-	-	1	1	2
551-600	-	-	3	-	3
over 600	1	-	1	-	2
Total	6	1	18	8	33

Source: TECS, 1984.

profit of Rs 52 per tonne on account of open market sales (Table 3.5).

Trends in the profitability of the cement industry as a whole can be examined from Figure 3.2 (derived from Table 8 of the Appen-

Table 3.5. Margins earned from cement production in 1982/3 (Rs per tonne)

Cost of production[1]	425.98
Levy realization[1]	330.51
Margin (levy)	−86.47
Non-levy realization	704.75
Margin (non-levy)	278.77
Average realization	478.46
Overall margin	52.48

Source: Cement Manufacturers' Association.
[1] Cost and realization figures are weighted averages for 47 units.

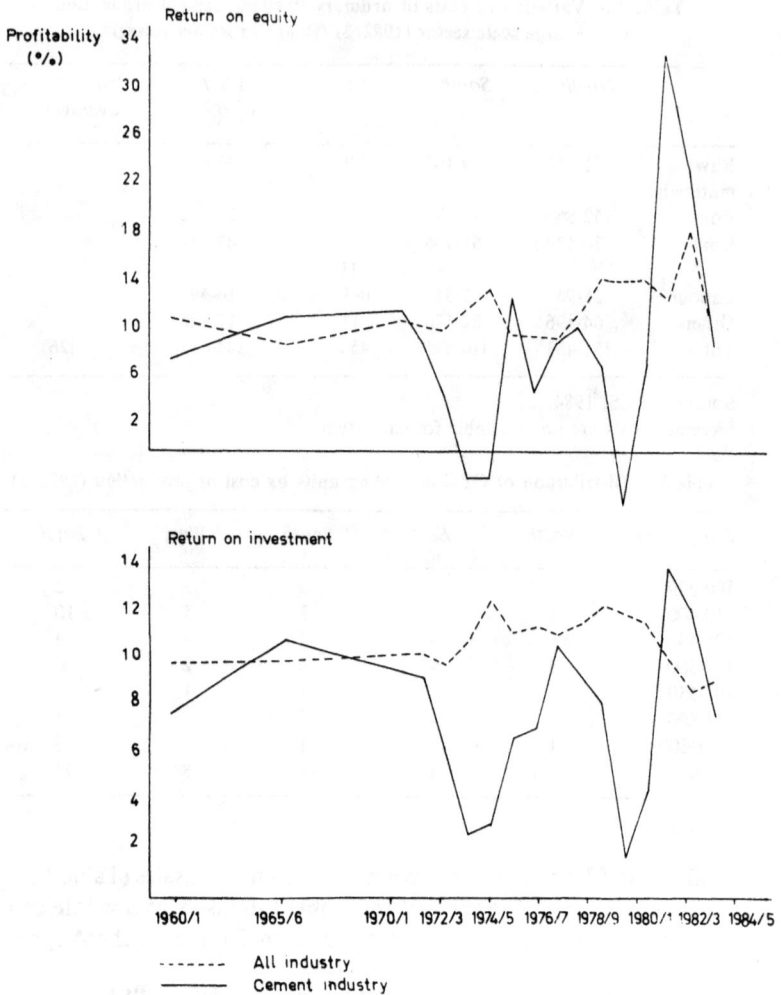

Figure 3.2 Profitability in cement industry

dix). A number of features emerge. Profitability was generally higher
during the period of cost plus pricing employed until the late 1960s
than during the uniform price regime which followed. The profitability of the cement industry was comparable with that of all Indian
industry until 1971/2 with returns on net worth averaging 10 to 11
per cent. During the restrictive regime of the mid-1970s this profitability declined considerably below that of all industry. In 1972/3
and 1973/4 the cement sector even registered a net loss. A recovery

in the late 1970s was followed by a sharp decline in subsequent years until the introduction of partial decontrol increased returns to 24 to 33 per cent, the highest ever. It is interesting to note that during the entire period from 1960/1 to 1981/2 the cement industry never achieved the average returns of 14 per cent on capital employed apparently allowed for in the calculation of retention prices. Even the allowance of 12 per cent on net worth suggested by the BICP was not achieved after its apparent implementation.

Another side effect of government intervention has been the shift from the production of OPC to PPC (Table 1.4). This has come about largely on account of the failure to differentiate in price fixing between the two types of cement. *A priori* the cost of producing PPC is likely to be less than that of producing OPC. Given the extreme interplant variations in production costs, however, it is difficult to present very concrete evidence on this. Nevertheless, the figures in Table 3.6 do suggest a greater bunching of plants in the lower cost ranges for PPC than for OPC. The fixing of separate retention prices since 1982 for levy cement may have reversed the trend to increased PPC production to some extent but its effect has been largely vitiated by the failure of the open market up to now to discriminate significantly between the two types.

Cement availability

As discussed earlier, government policy in India has affected cement availability through its effect on the rate of new investment

Table 3.6. Cost of production (1982/3)

Range/tonne	OPC/Slag		PPC	
	No of units	Cumulative proportion (%)	No of units	Cumulative proportion (%)
Below Rs 300	1	2.3	1	3.7
Rs 301 - 350	5	13.6	5	22.2
Rs 351 - 400	10	36.4	6	44.4
Rs 401 - 450	6	50.0	8	74.1
Rs 451 - 500	13	79.5	4	88.9
Rs 501 - 550	2	84.1	1	92.6
Rs 551 - 600	4	93.2	1	96.3
Rs 601 - 650	1	95.5	-	-
Above Rs 650	2	100.0	1	100.0

Source: CMA, 1984.

in the industry, capacity utilization and through inefficiencies in the
location of productive capacities relative to the consuming markets.
The impact of retention prices allowed to producers on the rate of
capital formation since 1970/1 can be seen from Table 3.7 and Figure
3.3. The low relative producer prices available to all units until 1976/7
are reflected in extremely low rates of increase in installed capacity
until 1978/9.

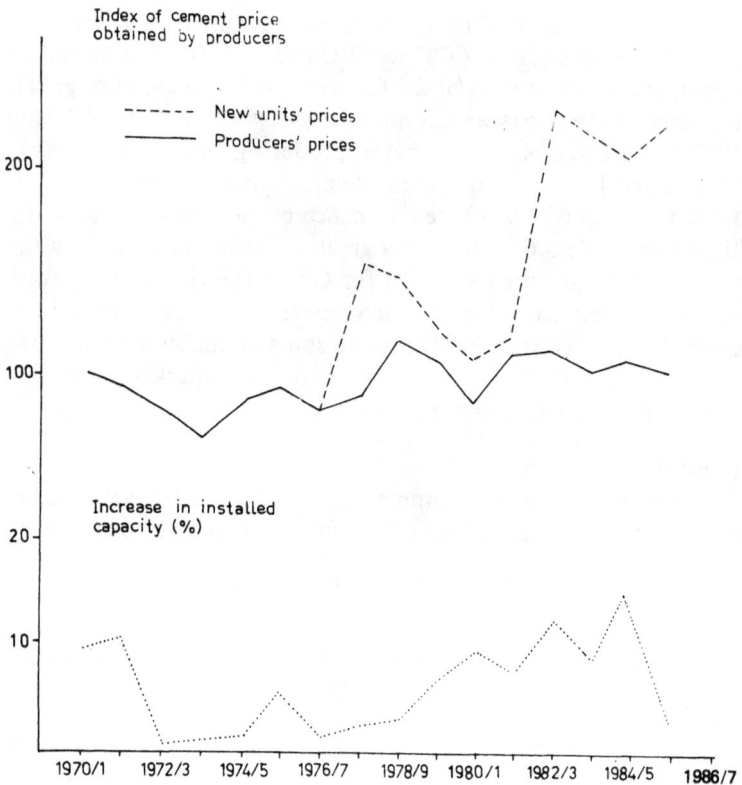

Figure 3.3 Producer prices and the rate of capital formation in the cement industry

Improved prices granted to new units from 1977/8 begin to be
translated into improved rates of increase in installed capacity in
1979/80 and 1980/1. Increased realization on non-levy sales since
1982/3 are now beginning to have an effect in terms of even higher
increases in installed capacity. These time lags are consistent with

Table 3.7. Impact of producer prices on capital formation and capacity utilization

Year	Installed capacity (m tonnes)	Annual increase in installed capacity (m tonnes)	% increase in installed capacity	Production (m tonnes)	Capacity utilization (%)	Relative price of cement to producers (1970/1 = 100)	
1956/6	12.0	0.76	6.8	10.58	88	113	
1970/1	17.61	1.63	10.2	14.35	81	100	
1971/2	19.56	1.95	11.1	15.07	77	93	
1972/3	19.76	0.20	1.1	15.55	79	83	
1973/4	19.76	-	-	14.66	74	71	
1974/5	20.06	0.30	1.5	14.80	74	89	
1975/6	21.16	1.10	5.5	17.29	82	94	
1976/7	21.46	0.30	1.4	18.84	88	84	
1977/8	21.91	0.45	2.1	19.38	88	93	156[1]
1978/9	22.25	0.64	2.9	19.42	86	119	149
1979/80	24.29	1.74	7.2	17.69	73	107	123
1980/1	26.99	2.70	10.0	18.56	69	90	110
1981/2	29.25	2.26	7.7	21.06	72	113	120
1982/3	33.51	4.26	12.7	23.30	70	115	230
1983/4	36.91	3.40	9.2	27.00[2]	73	104	220
1984/5	42.50	5.59	15.1	30.17[3]	71	111	210
1985/6	43.75[5]	1.25	2.9	33.10[4]	76	104	226

Sources: WGR, 1984 and Table 3.6

[1]From Table 3.2

[2]Provisional

[3]*Financial Express*, 10 July 1985

[4]*Financial Express*, 9 April 1986

[5](Actual) *Financial Express*, 25 March 1986

the two-to-four-year gestation periods common to new investment in the cement industry. These figures also correlate well with the variations in profitability seen in Figure 3.1.

Though variations in capacity utilization have a significant effect on profitability, they can only partly be correlated with the price regime in the Indian situation. An analysis of the effects of infrastructural shortcomings in the Indian economy on production in the cement industry (Figure 3.4) shows the dominance of this constraint. Generally, with a declining capacity utilization, there tends to be an increasing influence of infrastructural shortages (with minor exceptions) relative to that of the other constraints. Between 1976 and

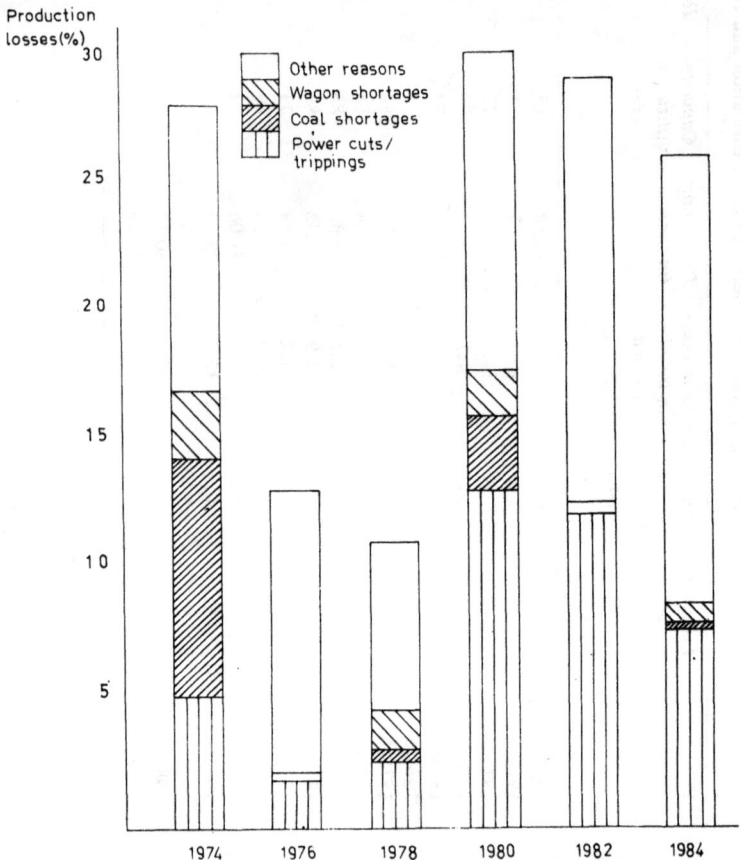

Figure 3.4 Major constraints on capacity utilization

1978, with capacity utilization at 87 to 89 per cent, the average loss on account of power, coal and wagon shortages was just 28 per cent of the total unused capacity. Between 1980 and 1982 the loss on this account had doubled to over 55 per cent, while capacity utilization had fallen to 70 per cent. The effect of these infrastructural short-comings on capacity utilization are illustrated in Figure 3.4.

It would appear from this that the effect of the price regime on capacity utilization was limited to the older plants. In their case, capital payments are less important than operational expenses, as a result of which the operating losses (if any) would be high when capacity utilization was high. For newer plants, lower operational expenses create an incentive for high capacity utilization in order to maximize the operational surplus available to cover capital payments.[a]

As originally conceived, the dual pricing policy provided an incentive to manufacturers to maximize capacity utilization. Only the production *above* a threshold proportion of capacity installed was allowed to be sold in the open market. In order to reduce the effect of power shortages, producers with in-house generation capacity were allowed to sell an increased proportion of the total additional production achieved as a result on the open market. Old units with captive power were allowed to sell 48.5 per cent of additional production as non-levy (instead of 33.4 per cent) and new units 61.3 per cent instead of 50 per cent.[b]

In March 1985 however, the basis of the dual pricing policy was changed from proportion of installed capacity to that of actual production.[c] The penal effect of this on efficient units (with over 100 per cent utilization) relative to those achieving lower levels of utilization have now been neutralized by allowing these units to sell a much higher proportion of output on the open market.

Transport and distribution

The discussion in Chapter 1 provided an indication of the extent of the need to transport cement over long distances. In order to com-

---

[a] As indicated earlier, the possibility of the greatly enhanced excise rates having become a factor in the low *reported* capacity utilization in recent years can also not be ruled out.
[b] *Cement*, Jan-Mar 1983.
[c] *Financial Express*, 5 June 1985.

pensate consumers in the deficit regions, a freight pooling system
has been in operation. This has enabled levy cement to be supplied
at a uniform FOR price throughout the country. The policy,
however, has a number of distortionary effects on the cement
economy.

A major problem with the policy of freight equalization has been
the shifting of the burden of transport costs from individual producers to the level of a cess borne uniformly by the industry as a
whole. As emphasized earlier, this is likely to have affected the investment decision away from the consideration of location of markets
largely to that of operating costs by increasing the concentration of
production in the limestone-abundant south and west to the neglect
of the northern markets and adding to the burden already imposed
on the transport system on account of the need to transport coal
over distances of 1,000 km and more. Table 9 of the Appendix shows
the average freight incurred in transporting cement within each region
as well as without in 1984. The average freight cost at the time constituted as much as 16 per cent of the FOR price of cement covering
an average distance of 700-800 km. Although this proportion has
been constant over a number of years, it is likely to be significantly
higher than it ought to be.

The actual magnitude of freight costs incurred on account of inter-
regional transport is illustrated in Figure 3.5. The significant features
are the movements of cement from the south and west to the north.
Table 1 of the Appendix provides an indication of the extent to which
cement prices in each state are distorted on account of freight
equalization. In average terms, cement is underpriced by about 3
per cent in the northern states and overpriced by nearly 5 per cent
in the south. In the absence of freight equalization, if production
were more rationally distributed, one might assume that northern
and western freight could be reduced substantially to, say, western
and southern levels respectively, suggesting that cement is over-priced
in the two regions by 5 per cent and 3 per cent respectively. The
potential for cement production in the east is very limited and it is
highly unlikely that significant savings in freight costs could be ef-
fected. It is clear from this analysis, however, that a significant
resource cost is imposed on the economy by the freight equalization
system. The resources wasted on this account amount to roughly
Rs 4.15 crores or 2.5 per cent of total freight costs.

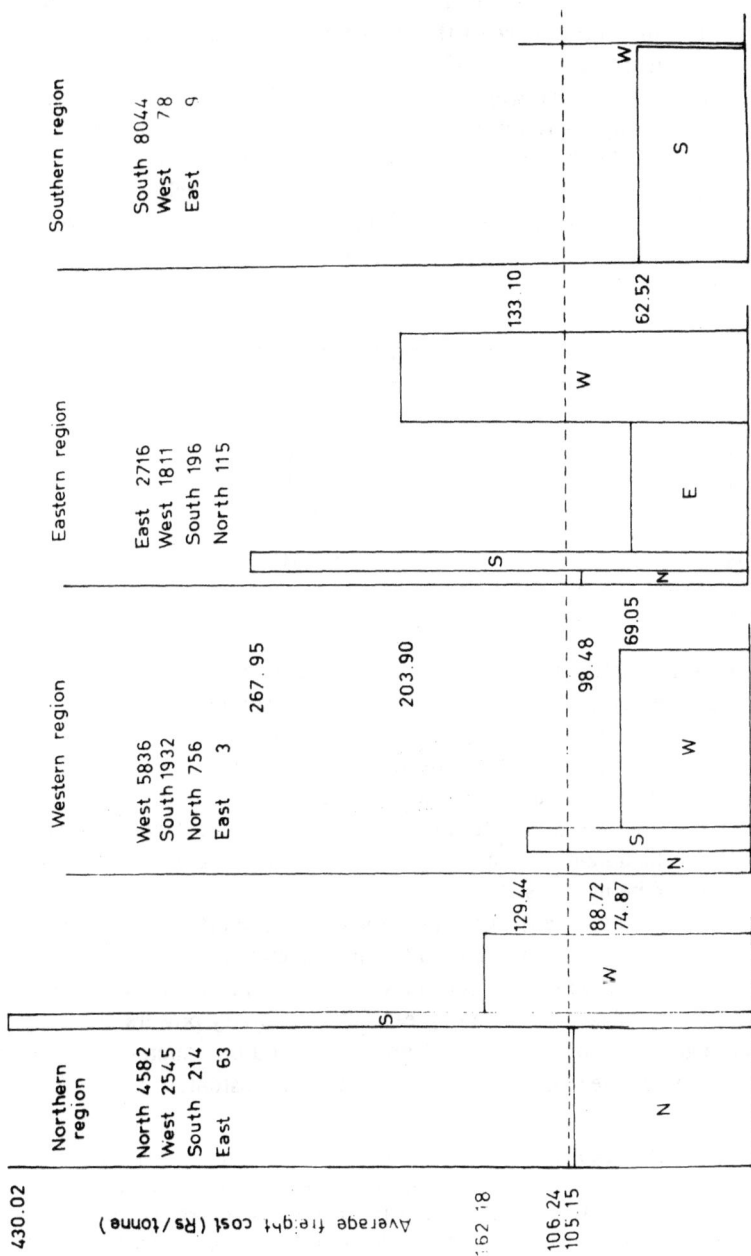

Figure 3.5 Average freight costs and cement quantities transported among regions

Quantities of cement transported to each region from alternative sources ('000 tonnes)

Average freight cost (Rs/tonne)

Northern region

North 4582
West 2545
South 214
East 63

Western region

West 5836
South 1932
North 756
East 3

Eastern region

East 2716
West 1811
South 196
North 115

Southern region

South 8044
West 78
East 9

430.02
267.95
203.90
133.10
129.44
98.48
88.72
74.87
69.05
62.52
106.24
105.15

One indication of the burden imposed upon the transport system is the decline in the share of the railways in cement transport from 80 per cent in the 1960s to 50 per cent today. Another indicator is the failure of the railways to make available to the industry the number of wagons required by it for the transport of cement. According to Table 3.8, just 80 per cent of the indented wagons were received by the industry in 1984. The effect of this will have been to increase the quantities of cement moved by more expensive road transport. The average freight incurred will naturally be higher than it would otherwise be.[a]

Table 3.8. Availability of railway wagons for transport of cement (1984)

Zone	Wagons indented	Received	Per cent
North	143,777	117,107	78.7
South	211,122	193,086	91.5
East	63,241	51,490	81.4
West	394,390	295,665	75.0
Total	817,530	657,348	80.4

Source: CCO, 1984.

Another distorting effect of this system, as shown earlier, is to reduce the economic price of cement to consumers in the deficit regions, thereby enhancing consumption in these regions while dampening consumption elsewhere. However, the extent to which this distortion is a valid consideration in a developing economy is arguable. Balanced development inevitably requires some inter-regional subsidization. The freight equalization system is now in the process of being phased out.

In addition to the distortions imposed by the attempt to ensure price parity throughout the country have been the problems caused by the attempt to ensure the pursuit of national priorities in the availability of cement. The degree of discretionary powers granted to the government consisting of politicians and bureaucracy, in the allocation of the ORC category is, of course, substantial. Before the

[a] It could be argued that the shortage of railway wagons is in fact the result of a failure to charge the correct economic price for railway transport. The freight burden imposed by increased road transport would then merely be a correction of this distortion. However, given the well known inefficiencies in the railway system, it is unlikely that the real subsidy in railway freight is very great.

introduction of dual pricing this was supplemented in most states by licensing powers for the public sale category. Final allocations for private consumption were made at the district and block levels. With open (black) market prices ruling at three to four times the levy price (particularly in large metropolises like Bombay) these discretionary powers became the source of considerable controversy with allegations of widespread corruption to the extent that many ruling politicians were said to have developed a vested interest in the shortages. The matter culminated in the downfall of the then Maharashtra Chief Minister, indicted for allegedly showing favours to big builders in the allocation of cement in exchange for large donations to 'trusts' established by him. To sum up, the control system generated exactly the phenomenon that Gunnar Myrdal had observed:

> When during and after World War II Western countries had to rely on a plethora of discretionary controls, black markets proliferated and corruption spread in spite of their very superior administrative machinery and personnel. There is a circular causation with cumulative effects in the sense that a corrupt body of administrators and politicians will have an interest in preserving and building up discretionary controls that give them the opportunity to enrich themselves.

This subsidy control system could also be seen in terms of the rent, seeking propertied classes being increasingly subsidized by the state (Bardhan, 1984). While the state in India produces 18 to 20 per cent of cement available through public sector companies, it also holds substantial interests in other companies through the share holdings of public sector financial institutions (25 to 45 per cent).

Alternative cementitious materials

In a developing country, the path of social modernization which evolves in the short to medium term often serves to exacerbate economic inequities and imbalances. There is evidence to suggest that this may be the case in terms of influences on the demand for cement amongst other effects. Amongst the alternatives to cement, lime-surkhi[a] and lime-ash combinations are well known in India.[b] The former, in particular, constitutes the primary binder for most

---

[a]Pulverized fire clay or brick-earth.
[b]See Spence, 1974 for a discussion of lime-surkhi manufacture in India.

historical monuments and old buildings. Since the nineteenth century it has also been used for canal and dam works apparently because of its lower shrinkage, greater impermeability and better ability to take internal stress than cement-based mortars.

There are no authoritative figures on the demand for and availability of alternative cementitious materials in India, as the materials are produced almost exclusively in the unorganized sector. It is the general simplicity of manufacture of these combinations which renders them suitable for the unorganized sector and also facilitates their widespread availability.[a]

The costs of cement and alternative mortars are compared in Table 3.9. It is clear from this that even the lime-surkhi combination is substantially cheaper (30 per cent) than an equivalent volume of cement mortar in the 1:6 combination (at current prices). The lime-ash combination enables an even greater saving (in excess of 40 per cent). It is only if cement is used in the weak 1:10 combination com-

Table 3.9. Alternative cementitious materials

Material	Quantity	Price (Rs)	Rate (Rs/cft)
Ash	350 cft	890	2.54
Surkhi	200 cft	600	3.00
Lime	1 quintal[b] (4.5 cft)	50	11.11
Cement	50 kg (1.5 cft)	66	44.90
Sand	350 cft	700	2.00

Building use

Combination (parts)	Cost (Rs/100 cft)
Surkhi (2) - Lime (1)	570
Ash (3) - Lime (1)	468
Cement (1) - Sand (6)	813
Cement (1) - Sand (10)	590

Source: Local market survey, Lucknow, April 1985.

[a] Despite fairly large requirements of capital (working capital, in particular), brick kilns are still allowed to hire most of their workers on a casual basis and thus escape the rigid and expensive provisions of the labour laws. It is a tribute to the political clout of the kiln owners that despite repeated attempts to discipline them, most recently in 1983, the government has failed to do so thus far.

[b] quintal—100 kg, cft cubic feet.

mon (but usually not legal) in contract building and government work that its cost begins to be comparable with that of other materials.[a] For private housing and industrial building, for which open market cement is used almost exclusively, alternative materials are considerably cheaper. Nevertheless, it is well known that the marketing efforts of the CMA in the early years were so successful that cement remains the preferred material. It is viewed by the consumer as superior to the other materials to the extent that, due to the cement shortage, building programmes have been postponed in the past rather than utilizing alternative materials. Evidence of this (from a micro-level survey) is presented in Chapter 6. It was only at the height of the

Table 3.10. Cement consumption in India (m tonnes)

Fiscal year	Production	Export	Import	Consumption[1]	% Growth[2]
1963-4	9.36	0.06	0.03	9.33	8.6
1965-6	10.58	0.04	-	10-54	6.2
1967-8	11.30	0.05	-	11.25	3.3
1969-70	13.00	0.16	-	13.64	10.1
1971-2	15.07	0.25	-14.80	4.2	
1973-4	14.66	0.20	-	14.46	(1.2)
1974-5	14.80	0.18	-	14.62	1.1
1975-6	17.29	0.54	-	16.75	14.6
1976-7	18.84	0.72	-	18.12	8.2
1977-8	19.38	0.77	0.21	18.82	3.9
1978-9	19.42	-	1.65	21.07	12.0
1979-80	17.69	-	1.80	19.49	(7.5)
1980-1	18.56	0.07	1.97	20.46	5.0
1981-2	21.06	-	1.60	22.66	10.8
1982-3	23.30	-	1.54	24.84	9.6
1983-4	27.07	neg	2.34	29.41	18.4
1984-5	30.17	0.03	0.46	30.60	4.0
1985-6	33.1[3]				

Sources: CCO various; Cement, 1984.
[1] Production + Import - Export.
[2] Annual basis.
[3] F.E. 9 April, 1986.

[a] It is worth noting, however, that these costs and prices are applicable to the urban Lucknow market. In rural markets, located close to lime/surkhi kilns, this combination is likely to be even cheaper.

Table 3.11. Per capita consumption of cement in selected countries

Industrialized countries	Per capita consumption (kg.) 1983
U.S.S.R.	470
Japan	678
U.S.A.	269
Italy	700
Federal Republic of Germany	481
France	448
Spain	816
U.K.	241
Developing countries	
India	35
China	93
Thailand	147
Pakistan	44
Morocco	174
Malaysia	268
Kenya	73
Sri Lanka	31
Burma	9

Source: CCO, 1974.

cement shortage in 1979 and 1980 that demand for the alternatives picked up to some extent.

The reluctance to use alternative cementitious materials (along with a marked failure to discriminate between OPC and PPC) is a remarkable feature of the Indian market situation. It bears considerable significance in the context of the demand for the output of mini-cement plants, and is discussed in Part II.

CHAPTER 4

Mini-scale Cement Production in India

Under the rules of the industrial promotion system in India, all plants with a capacity of 200 tonnes per day or less are classified as mini-cement plants (MCPs). In order to take advantage of the concessions allowed to MCPs, a number of rotary kiln plants have been established over the past few years with a nominal capacity of 200 tonnes per day. Despite the official classification of these plants as MCPs, however, it is well known that, at present levels of technology, it is not economically feasible to build/rotary kiln with a capacity of less than 300 tonnes per day. Accordingly, this discussion focusses on the vertical shaft kiln (VSK) mini-cement plant, while still recognizing the capacity created by rotary plants.

The rationale

In considering whether mini-scale cement production is suitable in developing countries in general and India in particular, the rationale behind encouraging the building of such plants must be borne in mind. This rationale is extensive and includes some factors specific to the cement industry and others more general to the development of appropriate technologies. The major arguments, based on Garg and Bruce, 1980 and CRI, 1983, are:

- the utilization of scattered small deposits of suitable quality raw materials, including limestone, marl and kankar, for cement production
- reduced burden on the transport infrastructure on account of a reduced market radius
- reduced packing and distribution costs due to the possibility of selling upacked cement directly to local consumers

- the possibility of producing a variety of cementitious products to suit local needs and of utilizing certain waste materials or products for productive purposes
- lower capital investment per unit capacity (lower capital-ouput ratio)
- greater employment per unit of investment (lower capital-labour ratio)
- a shorter gestation period (1 year) than in the case of large-scale plants (ranging from 2 to 5 years)
- dispersal of production to more rural locations, enabling more balanced regional development through employment creation and local product availability
- enabling persons of relatively limited means to undertake investment in the industry, and
- the reduced need for skilled personnel for operating sophisticated workshops for manufacturing the relatively simple machinery required for small plants.

Historical development in India

The VSK technology for mini-scale cement production is a development of the nineteenth century lime kiln. It was superseded in the early twentieth century for Portland cement production by the rotary kiln because of the possibility of operating the latter continuously, resulting in improved fuel efficiency and better uniformity and quality. VSK went out of use until the 1930s when interest in it was revived and new designs suitable for continuous rather than batch operation were developed. These were widely used in Germany during World War II and have continued to be used in Europe since, for a small proportion of cement production.[a] However, in recent years they have increasingly been phased out, the last VSK in Germany having stopped production in 1983. Nevertheless, they have continued to be used in Spain and Australia, in large numbers in China and, increasingly, in India.

While the Indian experience will be dealt with in detail in the following discussion it is interesting to note here that cement production in China more than tripled from 15 m tonnes in 1965 to 48 m tonnes in 1975. By 1983 it had reached 100 m tonnes. In 1975, 28.3 m tonnes (nearly 60 per cent) was produced in VSKs. By 1983,

[a]Spence, 1979.

this had increased to 81 m tonnes (75 per cent), the product of 4,800 mini-cement plants (MCPs).[a]

In India, experimental trials on the VSK started in 1948 at the Sangli works of the Deccan Cement Co. This resulted in the development in 1967 of a batch type kiln using part oil and part coal as fuel. The product, however, was equivalent to natural rather than Portland cement and could not be marketed successfully, so the project had to be dropped.[b]

Faced with the problem of transporting cement to inaccessible areas, the Ministry of Defence decided to sponsor the development of a 25 to 30 tonnes per day MCP. Having installed and tested a prototype kiln at Muradnagar, however, the ministry lost interest in the project and offered it to the state governments to build a complete pilot plant. The Tamil Nadu government built the plant under the supervision of the Army engineer, Major Ramachandran. However, the capital cost was fairly high and, although the plant did produce Portland cement, it could not be run successfully on a commercial basis.

This pilot plant at Muduvathur was later transferred to the Cement Research Institute of India (CRI) which claims to have completed its R&D work on the kiln 'after running the plant successfully for over six years'.[c] At the same time, Dr M S Iyenger of the defence department design team continued research on VSKs on becoming Director of the Regional Research Laboratory (RRL) at Jorhat (Assam). His emphasis was on smaller capacity kilns down to 1 tonne per day. These kilns were tested to a laboratory scale and the patents were handed to the National Research Development Corporation for commercial exploitation.

In 1965, the Planning Research and Action Institute of the Uttar Pradesh state government, initiated research on the basis of the design of the Defence Ministry VSK under the supervision of Mr M K Garg. The initial research and much subsequent effort was not successful and the plant was shut down in 1972. Interest in the project was revived in the late 1970s by M K Garg, now working under the aegis of the Appropriate Technology Development Association,

---

[a]Li et al. 1984. Of these 169 were rotary kiln plants—average 66,000 tonnes p.a.
[b]Garg and Bruce, 1980.
[c]CRI 1983, p vii.

Lucknow, and a project proposal was prepared.[a] Work based on the proposal was started in 1981 and is now nearing conclusion.[b]

Technologies and designs

Despite the profitable operations of VSKs in a number of developed countries many technologists still doubt the viability of the technology in terms of quality and consistency in operation. These technical doubts are discussed in terms of the characteristics of the technology by Stewart (1985):

> The vertical kiln is extremely simple in concept. In its solid fuel form, it consists of a vertical refractory-lined cylinder with solid fuel and limestone fed into the top of the kiln and combustion air fed into the bottom. A grate for removal of clinker is fitted at the bottom. In operation, it may be thought of as a combustion zone and two heat exchange zones. Solids entering the top of the kiln are heated by hot combustion gases until they reach combustion temperature in the fire zone. Below the fire zone, solids are cooled by incoming combustion air. In this way, a substantial amount of heat is recovered from both solids and gases before they leave the kiln. Because of this the inherent energy efficiency is normally better in a vertical kiln than that in a rotary kiln even when the latter is much larger; 3.63×10^9 joule/t has been quoted for vertical kilns of 66,000 tonnes per annum (Kirk Othmer, 1964) while even the most modern dry process rotary kilns with suspension preheater will use $5,3 \times 10^9$ joule/t (US Bureau of Mines, 1979) and the older type wet process rotary kiln considerably more (Spence, 1980).
>
> The problems of uneven heating and movement through the kiln that plagued the early vertical kilns have been largely overcome in modern vertical kilns by the use of a pelletized feed, incorporating the correct amount of fuel into the pellets of raw meal. With a pelletized feed of uniform particle size, there is a uniform resistance to gas flow across the bed and channelling is unlikely to occur. Accumulations of solid fuel and thus 'hot spots' cannot occur as each pellet contains its own correctly proportioned amount of fuel and in fact very uniform heating of the solid oc-

[a]Garg and Bruce, 1980.
[b]The subsequent history of the plant at Mohanlaganj and an analysis of its economics is contained in the following chapter.

curs. With modern refractories, problems of reaction with the walls and 'hang up' are eliminated (Gottlieb, 1973). The incorporation of the fuel into the pellets also appears to offer a further advantage. In vertical kilns using discrete particles of fuel, it is said to be necessary to use a fuel of low reactivity, such as metallurgical coke, to minimize the loss of fuel values caused by the reaction between carbon dioxide and carbon to produce carbon monoxide above the fire zone. This reaction represents a loss of fuel values and possibly a source of instability in kiln operation. Presumably the reduction in gas-solid fuel contact when the fuel is incorporated into the pellets reduces the importance of this effect and a vertical kiln plant in Australia has operated successfully for many years using brown coal char, a carbon source of high reactivity. This opens the way for the use of wood charcoal as a fuel in such kilns, although this has yet to be demonstrated in practice.

Stewart concludes that a properly designed and operated VSK is fully capable of producing cement of equal quality to that produced by a rotary kiln and cites the example of an Australian kiln which has, for many years, produced cement for optical applications such as offshore drilling rigs and power station construction. Both Stewart and Taubmann (1985) emphasize the need for careful operational control requiring skilled personnel if high standard quality cement is to be produced in VSKs. To some extent, the lower level of mechanization has to be compensated for by more skilled labour and more careful management.

Worldwide, while the VSK technology has been found to be feasible at varying scales from as little as 1 tonne per day up to 300 tonnes per day, the rotary kiln is generally regarded as efficient at capacities above 300 tonnes per day or 100,000 tonnes p.a.

In India, there are four organizations claiming to have developed the technology for MCPs. The Cement Research Institute of India, now known as National Council for Cement and Building Materials (NCB), the Regional Research Laboratory, Jorhat, a Jodhpur-based technologist-entrepreneur, D P Saboo and the ATDA. It needs to be clearly understood at the outset that there is extremely limited validity in these claims. They are all offering modified designs of VSKs in combination with materials handling, grinding, packing and pollution control systems of varying degrees of sophistication and capacity. None of these combinations and designs can, strictly, be said to be radically different from those in use in Europe or China. At best, therefore, it is the specific design in use which can be attributed to a particular claimant rather than a title to a radically new technology. While the first three offer a black meal process involving the mixing of raw materials before grinding and blending, the ATDA offers a semi-white meal intermixing process.

The NCB design

The NCB has emerged in recent years as the major claimant to the title of 'Developer of MCP Technology', despite being commonly regarded as being beholden to the large scale sector.[a] Yet it is widely understood that the Institute's contribution is limited to the design of the kiln to the virtual exclusion of the 'peripheral' equipment.[b] It is the machinery manufacturers licensed by the NCB who have worked on the development of materials handling, grinding systems and other peripheral machines as part of the technology packages offered by them to the entrepreneur. The machine configuration offered by one of the leading NCB licensees consists of a sophisticated technology package incorporating substantial automatic materials handling, heavy duty equipment of excellent quality and considerable electronic controls.

The RRL design

As indicated earlier, the main thrust of the RRL's research was on proving the feasibility of the technology for micro-scale production—as low as 1, 2 and 4 tonnes per day as well as the more conventional MCP capacities of 30 and 100 tonnes per day. Their work also appears to have been restricted to kiln design rather than the development of a technology package. The design is being exploited commercially by the NRDC.

The Saboo system

The Saboo design for cement production is based on a refinement of a prototype kiln developed from literature emanating from RRL, Jorhat. However, Sri Saboo claims considerable R&D work affecting the entire process including materials handling, grinding mills,

---

[a]This statement is based on personal interviews with cement technologists as well as machinery suppliers.
[b]The NCB relies on a levy of 75 paise per tonne of cement produced for 50 per cent of its funds. Of the rest, half consists of sponsorships by industry for research projects.

pollution and quality control systems in addition to kiln design. He thus offers (through his machine fabrication unit) a 'completely redesigned' technological package suited to the needs of relatively small investors with restricted access to sophisticated skills and repair workshops. He has not only reduced the cost considerably but also claims much lower power requirements per tonne of cement produced than for other large or small scale processes (see Chapter 5). Inevitably, this has reduced capital costs at the expense of technical sophistication. Equipment is significantly less durable than that offered by the NCB, much of the materials handling is manual and controls are rudimentary.

The ATDA plant

A major objective of the establishment of the ATDA pilot plant at Mohanlalganj (near Lucknow, Uttar Pradesh) was to develop a commercially viable mini-cement technology for manufacturing ISI grade OPC from local calcareous materials such as marl and kankar. After considerable R&D effort and a number of false starts, regular commercial production was started in February 1984 at Mohanlalganj, ISI certification for the product (conforming to IS269: 1976 for OPC) was received in March 1984, and IDBI approval for selective refinancing of plants based on the ATDA design was obtained in July 1984.

The technique developed at Mohanlalganj differs from the other MCP designs in intermixing rather than intergrinding the raw material with fuel. Coal is ground separately in the ATDA process and mixed with the raw meal at the blending (or homogenization) stage rather than for feeding to the raw mill. This necessitates a larger size of homogenizer than is used for other MCP designs but compensates for the higher capital cost in enabling greater flexibility in production. This semi-white meal (rather than black meal) process is reputed to be the one more suited to variable quality raw material as it enables frequent adjustments in the fuel feed. In the case of the marl-based design at Mohanlalganj, it also incorporates a rotary drier to reduce the moisture content from 8 to 20 per cent (when marl is mined) down to the required 0.5 per cent at the grinding stage. This enhances both capital and operational (power) costs in this case.

The period of commercial production at Mohanlalganj was supposed to generate operational information of an economic and financial as well as a technical nature. In retrospect, it has been recognised that the data obtained has been greatly affected by the age of the plant and the continuing need for modifications emerging from the exercise. The data obtained do, however, serve as a basis for reasonably accurate estimates of operating costs (and technical parameters) to be made for a first generation dissemination plant based on the ATDA design. This information is used for comparative purposes in Chapter 5.

Demand for MCPs

Against a background of cement shortage and the indulgent attitude of the government towards MCPs, the demand for this production facility blossomed between 1982 and 1984. Table 4.1 provides an indication of this demand. Between the commissioning of the first commercial VSK MCP in August 1981 and January 1986, nearly 60 MCPs had been commissioned in India (and one in Bhutan). According to the available information, at least 50 were on order. While Saboo, concentrating on 20-30 tonnes per day units, appears to be the most successful, one of the NCB licensees, purveying mainly 50 and 100 tonnes per day plants is also doing remarkably well. The RRL, Jorhat, has adopted a low profile but still sold a few plants. Owing to its late entry, the ATDA is yet to sell a plant based on its design.

Table 4.1. VSK mini-cement plants in India

| States | Plants in production | | | | |
	NCB/ Movers	Other NCB	Saboo	RRL Jorhat	Total
Andhra Pradesh	1	2	-	-	3
Arunachal Pradesh	1	-	-	-	1
Bihar	-	1			1
Gujarat	1	3	2	3	9
Himachal Pradesh	-	-	1	-	1
Jammu & Kashmir	-	1	1	-	2
Karnataka	4	2	-	-	6
Madhya Pradesh	3	2	2	-	7
Maharashtra	-	-	1	-	1
Orissa	1	-	1	-	2
Rajasthan	-	1	17	-	18
Tamil Nadu	1	1	-	-	2
Uttar Pradesh	-	1	3	-	4
Bhutan	1	-	-	-	1
Total (commissioned)	13	14	28	3	58
Plants on order	24	n a	22	4	50[1]

[1] According to the available information.

A quantification of future investment intentions is provided by figures on licences and registrations in Table 4.2. Units with a capacity of 200 tonnes per day are required to obtain an industrial licence although they are otherwise classified as MCPs. Units with a lower capacity are required only to register with the Directorate General of Technical Development (DGTD). By December 1984, 24 units of 200 tonnes per day capacity had been granted licences, having implemented a sufficient portion of their proposals to satisfy the government of future production. Another 59 proposed units had been granted 'letters of intent' for 200 tonnes per day plants. All these units/proposals will have been for rotary kiln-based plants. At least 9 other 200 tonnes per day plants were already in production.

As Table 4.2 shows, by mid 1984, 87 DGTD registrations had been granted for VSK plants, in addition to the 19 already in production. A majority of these were in the 31-99 tonnes per day range although with 100 tonnes per day units being promoted increasingly by the NCB, 40 per cent of the registrations were in the 100-200 tonnes per day range.

Table 4.2. Registration of mini-cement plants

States	*Industrial licences*	*Letters of Intent*	*Registrations with DGT*		
			30 TPD	*31-99 TPD*	*100-200 TPD*
Andhra Pradesh	7	2		2	2
Assam	-	4	1	1	1
Bihar	-	1	-	-	1
Gujarat	6	13	4	14	1
Haryana	-	1	-	-	-
Himachal Pradesh	-	7	1	5	5
Karnataka	5	11	-	5	9
Madhya Pradesh	2	5	1	8	7
Maharashtra	1	-	-	-	-
Orissa	-	2	-	2	-
Rajasthan	3	4	-	-	2
Uttar Pradesh		7	-	2	2
Jammu & Kashmir	-	-	-	3	3
Pondicherry	-	-	-	-	1
Tamil Nadu	-	-	-	2	1
Meghalaya	-	2	-	1	-
Total	24	59	7	45	35
Total Annual Capacity (m tonnes)	1.58	3.74		2.35	

Sources: WGR, 1984; CCO, 1984.

The total capacity creation implied by these licences and registrations amounts to 7.7 m tonnes with another 1.2 m tonnes of annual capacity already in production. Assuming that all this capacity materializes by the end of the Seventh Plan period (1989/90), the 8.9 m tonnes of MCP capacity will constitute roughly 11 per cent of the total available capacity.[a] The present MCP capacity of 1.2 m tonnes constitutes 2.6 per cent of the total capacity of 45.9 m tonnes.

So great has been the demand for the financing of MCPs that in January 1985 the Industrial Development Bank of India (IDBI) suspended its assistance schemes for MCPs. On the basis of applications received by then, the IDBI had sanctioned Rs 83.84 crores as direct assistance to 31 MCPs and Rs 52.67 crores as refinancing for 85 MCP projects.[b] It was stated at the time that this was on account of the large number of projects sanctioned on which concrete information of progress or realised viability was not available. After reconsideration, however, this policy appears to have been revised to assist small VSK units between 50 and 100 tonnes per day 'on a selective basis'.

An examination of the regional distribution of MCPs suggested by the figures in Tables 4.1 and 4.2 shows that a large proportion of the capacity will be located in Gujarat (20.3 per cent), Madhya Pradesh (12.8 per cent), Karnataka (21.3 per cent) and Rajasthan (7.6 per cent). As much of the large-scale sector capacity is also located in these states, this is unlikely to ease much of the burden on the transport infrastructure. Except in Rajasthan, it is also not clear to what extent the MCPs will be utilizing scattered deposits of limestone not otherwise suitable for large-scale production. To some extent, the 11 proposed MCPs in Uttar Pradesh and 17 in Himachal Pradesh will be utilizing smaller deposits as well as easing the cement deficit in the north, thereby justifying their existence in terms of two important macro-economic factors.[c] Plants in other states such as Jammu and Kashmir and the northeastern regions will also make a positive contribution in this respect.

---

[a] Capacity and numbers of plants constitute the best estimates possible as there is only varying and sometimes contradictory information available even within a single source (notably WGR, 1984).
[b] *Financial Express*, 9 July 1985.
[c] The fulfillment of the micro-economic rationale will be discussed in Chapter 6.

Dissemination

The dissemination strategy adopted by the 'developers' of MCP designs have incorporated a varying degree of involvement on their part. The RRL, Jorhat, lies at one extreme in this activity. Having licensed the NRDC for commercial exploitation of the design, the laboratory appears to take little further part in the dissemination exercise. Greater involvement in dissemination on the part of the CRI and Saboo warrants a more detailed description.

The NCB strategy

The NCB dissemination strategy has been to license machinery manufacturers with an established production capability to supply plant based on its design. As many as 16 machinery manufacturers have been licensed and are located in all the main regions of the country. As the NCB's main innovation is in kiln design, each manufacturer is effectively left to put together the 'peripherals' on their own. Perhaps partly as a result, not all the licensed machinery manufacturers have made equal efforts to market the product. Certainly the success achieved has been variable. One, originally a materials handling machinery manufacturer, has undertaken considerable innovation and introduced increasingly sophisticated materials, handling and instrumentation to become the market leader for the NCB design. The organization now derives an overwhelming proportion of its income from mini cement machinery. Two other organizations have also achieved some success.

The NCB provides support to its 'exclusive' licensees[a] in the form of feasibility studies, identification and surveys of raw material deposits and training of personnel. For this a consultancy fee is charged. Given the involvement of the NCB (a government sponsored organization) in a project it naturally becomes easier to obtain financial assistance from the 'public' financial institutions.

The Saboo system

Shri D P Saboo's Shree Engineers claim to have a very thorough approach to dissemination. According to them, their design incorporates all aspects of cement production including pollution control, quality control and the need to minimize the maintenance requirements of diverse rural-based entrepreneurs. They emphasize

[a] The NCB insists that its licensees do not deal with any other MPC 'technologies'.

that the key to success is close supervision by the entrepreneur or a close associate and the dissemination process is designed to weed out those unable to ensure this.

Initially, prospective investors in the Saboo package are sent a questionnaire designed to assess their awareness of the industry's requirements and the feasibility of their project. After agreement, they are expected to start hiring technical staff who are then trained by Saboo. Trainees are expected to do considerable homework before training and are appraised during the course of it.

Of the 28 Saboo-designed plants currently in operation, 17 are located in Rajasthan alone, whereas the others are spread all over the country. The concentration in Rajasthan is not only on account of the proximity of the machinery supplier but also due to better local publicity and the large number of small deposits of limestone in the state.

Government policy

The government's attitude to MCPs has been ambivalent. Ever since the emergence of these plants in the late 1970s as a commercial possibility in India, the government has felt duty-bound, in terms of its traditionally stated preference for small versus large, to assist them. Thus, as indicated earlier, the IDBI provides refinancing assistance to these plants but this is done only on the basis of certain restrictive guidelines and norms, which include:

- MCPs should be set up primarily to exploit limestone reserves in scattered pockets and also at places where it is difficult for large cement plants to be set up on a viable basis
- the mini plants should have adequate local markets in their vicinity to minimize transportation
- there should not normally be any large cement plant existing or proposed within a radius of 200 km except if the above conditions are fulfilled
- clustering of plants should be avoided as far as possible.

In addition, certain incentives in the form of concessions and assistance have been provided. MCPs have been exempted from distribution controls to enable them to take advantage of a smaller market radius by saving on freight costs. A 50 per cent relief from excise duty was also provided from 1978 to 1982. When excise was raised to Rs 135 per tonne in 1982 the concession was frozen at

Rs 35 per tonne. During 1983/4, the duty payable by MCPs was Rs 170 per tonne compared to Rs 205 per tonne for large plants. In 1984, however, this concession was withdrawn and all plants now pay Rs 225 per tonne. Complete price and distribution control exemption is thus now the only advantage in government policy towards MCPs.

The extent of the government's indulgence is restricted to this fiscal latitude—no concessions in terms of the physical and chemical properties of the output are allowed. In the context of MCPs, the government specifically issued a press note clarifying that:

> No person shall himself, or by any person on his behalf, manufacture or store for sale, sell or distribute cement which does not conform to the prescribed standard and which does not bear the 'ISI' Certification Mark.

The output of MCPs, like that of all cement plants, must conform in effect to one of the two main standards for OPC and PPC.

CHAPTER 5

Mini-cement Production:
An Economic Analysis

A comparison of the investment and production economics of the available designs for mini-cement production could serve two purposes—firstly, to enable an assessment of the economic efficiency of these techniques relative to each other and secondly, to enable an analysis of the extent to which the rationale for the reduced scale is justified. This chapter begins by examining relative costs within the mini sector and goes on to make some economic comparisons with figures available for the large-scale sector. The discussion of mini cement is largely restricted to the two main contending designs in the Indian MCP market, those of Saboo and the NCB. To the extent possible, the Mohanlalganj experience is used to add ATDA to the comparison.

Investment costs

A summary comparison of the costs of investment in VSK-based mini-cement plants is provided in Table 5.1. Figures for the Saboo design are based on Shree Engineers' quotes with figures for preoperative expenses being adjusted to make them more realistic in the opinion of the author. For the NCB technique, estimates for three scales of plant, 30, 50, and 100 tonnes per day have been provided. These are based on quotes obtained from one of the major NCB licensees.

The figures in the Table suggest fairly substantial scale economies in investment for each technique taken separately. As the Table shows, for each capacity of plant investment, costs for the NCB design offered by one of the leading suppliers (MPL) are substantially higher than for the Saboo design. Illustrated diagrammatical-

Table 5.1. Comparative summary of investment costs

(Rs. Lakhs)

	20 tpd Saboo	30 tpd Saboo	30 tpd NCB	50 tpd Saboo	50 tpd NCB	100 tpd Saboo	100 tpd NCB
Land	1.50	2.00	2.50	3.00	3.50	6.00	7.00
Building	19.13	23.44	26.25	34.65	39.21	49.77	55.17
Plant and machinery:							
Raw meal section	9.22	10.38	25.46	10.83	32.35	28.32	43.17
Nodulizer and clinkering section	7.50	9.28	19.47	10.48	18.45	25.43	29.31
Cement mill section	6.25	8.25	15.13	8.39	25.54	24.22	33.56
Electrical and instrumentation section	3.74	4.15	12.45	5.38	20.48	9.50	27.78
Freight and insurance	1.12	1.43	3.18	1.70	4.66	2.60	7.50
Technical erection & commissioning charges	2.85	3.25	15.00	5.75	23.00	8.00	30.00
Miscellaneous	3.08	3.14	3.25	4.85	4.00	4.92	4.50
Total (plant and machinery)	33.76	39.88	93.94	47.38	128.48	102.99	175.82
Preoperative expenses	5.00	7.00	7.00	9.00	9.00	13.00	13.00
Total fixed capital	59.39	72.32	129.69	94.03	180.19	171.76	250.99
Cost/installed annual tonne (Rs)[1]	990	804	1310	627	1092	573	761

[1] Assumes 330 normal working days per annum for NCB and 300 days for Saboo.

ly in Figure 5.1, the two sets of costs yield separate curves. Given the different levels of sophistication of the two techniques, this is inevitable.

It is also not surprising that the minimum economic scale (m.e.s.) in the case of Saboo is 50 tonnes per day while that for the NCB (MPL) design is in the region of 100 tonnes per day. Below these levels of output, investment costs per tonne rise steeply. Both the techniques at m.e.s. are economically efficient relative to the large scale sector which, even at its (currently) most efficient scale of 3,000

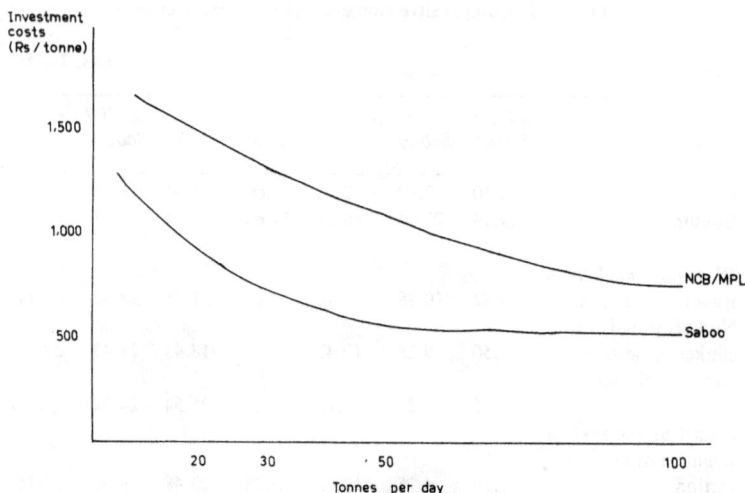

Figure 5.1 Economies of scale in investment (mini-cement)

tonnes per day, requires Rs 1,050 per annual installed tonne compared to Rs 760 for NCB (MPL) at 100 tonnes per day and Rs 570 for Saboo at 50 tonnes per day.[a]

Production costs

Data on costs of production was obtained from 20 tonnes per day units located in Rajasthan and Uttar Pradesh based on the Saboo design, a 100 tonnes per day unit based on the NCB design and located in Karnataka and the ATDA pilot plant at Mohanlalganj. As in the case of large cement plants, location is an important factor in production costs. The price of raw materials in particular is affected by location due to the varying incidence of transport costs on different items in various parts of the country. Thus, while the cost of coke breeze transported to MCPs in Rajasthan from Orissa or W. Bengal is high[b] the cost of locally mined gypsum is relatively low.[c] In Karnataka both coke breeze and gypsum are highly priced whereas in central Uttar Pradesh the cost of limestone is relatively

---

[a]Based on recently available figures for a 1.2 million tpa plant of Modi Cements and 0.75 million tpa plant of Madras Cement.
[b]Rs 700 per tonne compared to Rs 320 per tonne ex-steel plant (the seller).
[c]Rs 100 per tonne compared to Rs 330 per tonne in Karnataka.

high.[a] Individual cost variations of this type make direct comparisons between the performance of different types of plant design impossible.

The comparison of production costs presented for the three plant designs in Table 5.2 is based on information on specific consumption for each type of plant extracted from the data obtained from operating units. This has been 'normalized' for Uttar Pradesh conditions on the assumption that the plant would be located near a quarry in the south-eastern part of the region. Details of prices used and costs calculated are contained in Tables 11 a-c of the Appendix. An examination of Table 5.2 and the appendix tables yields the following observations:

Table 5.2. Mini-cement: a comparison of production costs (Rs/tonne)

Item	Design		
	Saboo (20)	ATDA (25)	NCB (100)
Raw materials	80.00	92.00	74.35
Coal	144.00	182.00	151.20
Power	117.00	179.22	152.05
Labour	81.17	70.40	25.82
Other production costs	154.23	158.17	163.85
Total direct costs	576.40	681.79	567.27
Capital cost[1]	223.85	156.44	117.76
Total cost	800.25	838.23	685.03

Source:
[1]Annualized: interest rate 13 per cent, seven year plant life for Saboo and 15 years for ATDA and NCB.

- there is no significant difference in direct production costs between the 20 tonnes per day Saboo design and the 100 tonnes per day NCB design. ATDA costs are significantly higher on account of the higher coal and power consumption entailed in the need to dry marl.[b] The lower labour costs of NCB are offset by the higher power consumption relative to Saboo. The latter's lower power costs, however, are related more to the relatively light (and,

[a]Rs 140 per tonne compared to Rs 45 per tonne if located near a quarry in southeast Uttar Pradesh.
[b]If the design was altered to use a limestone based inter-mixing process there are indications that the costs incurred would fall to levels similar to NCB and Saboo.

according to technical opinion, non-durable) machinery than to
technical sophistication
- the significantly lower labour costs of the NCB plant is a function largely of scale—total labour costs increase only marginally
  in increasing scale from 30 to 100 tonnes per day resulting in a
  significant reduction in unit costs
- on the basis of technical opinion, the *useful* life of the Saboo plant
  is taken as seven years and of the ATDA and NCB as 15 years.
  Capital costs are calculated on an annual basis by using the standard formula.[a] The prevailing back rate of 13 per cent on fixed
  capital yields an estimate of capital costs at market prices. The
  capital costs estimated in the Table are affected both by the scale
  factor (evident from Table 5.1) and by the different expected plant
  life. Here, the NCB plant at 100 tonnes per day emerges as clearly more economical than the ATDA plant and the 20 tonnes per
  day Saboo plant. The 15 per cent lower production cost of the
  NCB is a significant saving.

As Saboo has also quoted at 100 tonnes per day (though no plants
appear to have been established so far) it is only fair to make a comparison with NCB (100). This is done below on the assumption that
labour costs for Saboo will fall to similar levels as for NCB (100)
but other direct costs are more or less unaffected by scale:

Costs (Rs/tonne)	Saboo (100)	NCB (100)
Direct	521.05	567.27
Capital	129.56	117.76
Total	650.61	685.03

In this case, although the theoretical Saboo plant has lower costs, the
difference of 5 per cent is too low to be significant—small managerial
lapses would be sufficient to neutralize the difference. It must,
therefore, be concluded that in terms of economic efficiency at
market prices the Saboo and NCB designs are roughly on a par.

[a]Annualized capital cost = $\dfrac{Kr}{1 - \dfrac{1}{(1 + r)^n}}$

where K = capital cost per installed tonne
    r = rate of interest
    n = estimated life of plant

Sales realization

All the MCPs covered in the course of this study claimed to be enjoying a premium in the market of Rs 2-5 per bag of cement sold. In early 1985, market prices obtained by these units ranged from Rs 1,240-1,330 per tonne of cement. In early 1986 when the cement of large-scale producers (such as ACC) sold in the east Uttar Pradesh market at Rs 1,340 per tonne, a local MCPs' output was quoted at Rs 1,390.

While these prices and premiums are likely to be related to local factors (and variable with them) as much as to the costs of production, it is clear that despite their small scale these plants are able to differentiate their product so as to obtain a price higher than that prevailing in the open market. Local accountability, as well as stringent quality control, appear to be the key factors here.

Assuming an average 1984/5 price of Rs 1,280 per tonne, the net revenue to the plant can be obtained in the following way:

	Rs/tonne
Market price	1,280
Less: dealer's margin	30
transport cost	30
Ex-factory price	1,220
Less: excise duty	205
sales tax	75
selling and distribution	20
other levies[1]	10
Net revenue	900

[1] Contribution to CRA and NCB.

A comparison with the large-scale sector

Table 5.3 compares cost data for the most efficient 100 tonnes per day NCB plant with weighted average production cost data available for ten large sector cement companies in the private sector for 1984/5. These companies accounted for over 40 per cent of the total capacity and over 48 per cent of output in that year. Given their capacity utilization of 85 per cent (in a year when overall utilization was 71 per cent) they represent a relatively efficient segment of the large sector.

Table 5.3. A comparison with the large-scale sector (Rs/tonne)

	NCB (MPL)	Large scale[1]
Installed capacity (tpd)	100	1,575
Investment cost	761	1,050[2]
Sales realisation	900	720[3]
		(848)[4]
Production costs:		
Raw materials	74.35	108.44
Coal	151.20	
		201.39
Power	152.05	
Labour	25.82	45.03
Other	163.85	190.81
Total (direct)	567.27	545.67
Annual capital cost[5]	117.76	149.47
Total	685.03	695.14
IRR (%)[6]	43.5	12.8
		(22.5)

[1] Weighted averages for ten private sector companies in 1984/5.
[2] For a new plant 0.75-1.20 m tonnes p a.
[3] Actual including levy sales.
[4] Non-levy sales only.
[5] 13 per cent interest, 20 year life for large scale.
[6] MCP, one year gestation; large plant, three year gestation.

As the Table shows, while raw material costs are significantly higher for the large sector, power and fuel costs are very considerably lower. The high cost of raw materials to large plants is likely to be the result of a combination of relatively labour-intensive quarrying in the organized sector and the lack of selectivity in mining referred to earlier. Coal used by the large-scale sector for rotary kilns is ordinary non-coking coal which, in 1984, had an average price of Rs 183 per tonne. Low volatility coke breeze used by VSK MCPs, on the other hand, was priced at around Rs 320 per tonne (ex-Rourkela Steel Plant) at that time. This price difference is a major contributor to the difference in power and fuel costs. Another important factor is the considerable difference in captive power generation costs incurred by MCPs (using relatively small diesel generator sets) and the coal-based thermal or large diesel plants of the large sector.

The difference in labour costs between the two sectors is related to a relatively high requirement of skilled labour for the large sector as well as to the operation of a Cement Wage Board. The awards of the Wage Board are applicable to the large sector but not to MCPs. Thus, while minimum wages paid by the large sector are currently around Rs 1,100 those paid by MCPs are around Rs 300-350 per month.

The differences in other costs can only be attributed to the more complex management systems necessary for large sector operation, the need to maintain large headquarters and financial advisory staff and also, to some extent, to waste which is inherent to hired management in the large sector compared to the tight proprietorial control typical of MCPs.

The total direct costs shown in the Table are slightly higher for the MCP than for large scale. The difference of under 4 per cent, however, cannot be regarded as significant for an industry which shows a variation of 38.5 per cent in production costs.[a]

Annual capital cost for the two types of unit is calculated at the private interest rate for commercial borrowers (13 per cent) but with an expected life of 20 years for the large plant compared to 15 years for the MCP. The cost of nearly Rs 150 per tonne for large-scale production compared to under Rs 120 for MCP roughly equalizes the total costs of Rs 690 per tonne of cement (including packing charges) in 1984/5. It would appear from this calculation that, at market prices, there is no cost advantage to relatively efficient production in either sector.

In Table 5.3 internal rates of return (IRR) at market prices are also calculated. Since large sector sales realization (Rs 720 per tonne) is adversely affected by the levy obligation, the weighted average non-levy realization is used for an alternative calculation. The high IRR (43.5 per cent) of the MCPs relative to large scale is related to four factors:

- lower average capital cost
- lower gestation period—one year rather than three
- no levy obligation
- the apparent ability to realize higher prices on a quality assurance in a local market compared to the widespread market and large dealer network of the large sector. In a market in which adultera-

---

[a]calculated from data available for 46 units in TECS, 1984.

tion became an important issue in the years of shortage, the quality assurance of the small producer with a more easily controllable dealer network carries weight.[a]

Even without the levy obligation, IRR for the large sector only rises to 22.5 per cent.

Transport costs

Transport costs are usually cited as a major component of the rationale for MCPs. Information on costs of transport obtained for MCPs has been 'normalized' for the assumed Uttar Pradesh location and presented in Table 5.4. For the large-scale sector, estimates for transport costs derived from various sources are contained in Table 5.5.[b]

Table 5.4. Contribution of transport cost to the price of cement

Item	Transport costs	
	Rs/t of material	Rs/t of cement
Limestone	15	18.00
Clay	10	2.10
Coke breeze	380	79.80
Gypsum	180	9.00
Total raw material		108.90
Cement		30.00
Total transport cost		138.90
Transport cost of raw materials as % of direct production cost		19.2
Total transport cost as % of selling price		10.9

The main component of transport cost incurred by MCPs in most locations is that on account of fuel (coal) which has to be transported from steel plants (where it is a byproduct) to the cement plant. As the market radius is small (up to 150 km), the cost of cement

[a]In case of the emergence of a demand constraint in the market in the future this advantage may disappear. In 1986, many cement producers are already placing great emphasis on quality as a hallmark of their output and mounting publicity campaigns on that basis.
[b]All costs are for 1984/5.

Table 5.5. Transport costs incurred by large-scale sector

Item	Average distance from plant (km)	Average transport costs (Rs/t)	Consumption factor	Average transport costs/t of cement
Raw materials				
Limestone	26[1]	12[4]	1.25 – 1.30	15.00 – 15.60
Coal	1,000[2]	180[5]	0.28 – 0.32	50.40 – 57.60
Gypsum	1,200 – 1,500[3]	200 – 235[5]	0.05	10.00 – 11.75
Total raw materials				80.20
Transport costs as a % of production costs				14.7
Cement	650 (Rail)	165.60		
				115.58[6]
	200 (Road)	65.55		
Total transport costs				195.78
Total transport costs as a % of selling price				15.8

[1] Estimated from NCAER, 1979.
[2] WGR, 1984.
[3] Estimate based on location of gypsum producers.
[4] Rail and rope-way facilities owned by plant.
[5] Rail.
[6] Derived and updated from CCO, 1982 & WGR, 1984.

transport is low. For the large-scale sector, though coal transport is still an important component, it is the transport cost of cement which forms the bulk (59 per cent) of the total transport costs incurred, the average market radius being around 500 km.

Total transport costs incurred by large plants (around 16 per cent of selling price) are substantially higher than the 10 to 11 per cent incurred by MCPs. The transport saving from MCP operation can, therefore, be said to be significant if the plant is properly sited. The share of transport costs and taxes in the production cost and margin on cement is depicted in Figure 5.2.

NCB

Margin : Rs. 713
     transport 4%
     taxes 40%

Production cost Rs.567
     transport 19%

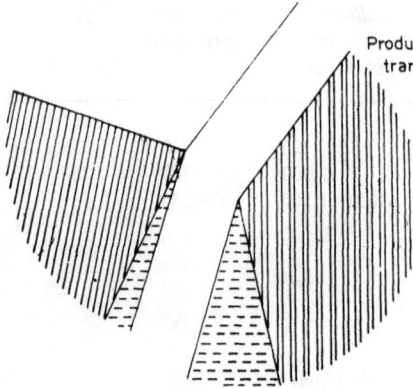

Large scale :

Margin : Rs. 694
     transport 17%
     taxes 41%

Production cost : Rs.546
     transport 15%

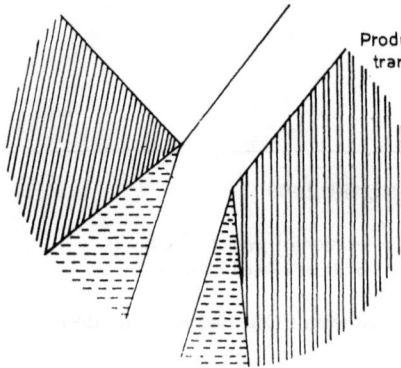

Figure 5.2   Distribution of transport costs and taxes in total costs

The economic valuation of cement

A well-established definition of economic value is its opportunity
cost or the landed cost of imported cement. In 1984 this amounted
to Rs 585 per tonne compared to the Rs 690 per tonne at market
prices calculated above. In order to obtain the true resource cost of
the cement, however, the effects of government regulation, taxes and
subsidies have to be allowed for. The following adjustments in
market prices need to be made.

Coal

The problem of coal quality (discussed in Chapter 2) is compensated for automatically in the cement industry in the necessity to use larger quantities per tonne of cement, in higher maintenance costs, particularly of captive thermal generation facilities and in the need to use limestone with a higher lime content. This, however, only aggravates the quantity problem.

The coal industry has lost over Rs 1,200 since nationalization in 1971. While there is dispute about the reasons for these losses, it is clear that the resource cost of the coal being consumed is usually substantially higher than that paid directly by the consumer. Information available on the finances of coal companies shows that the losses amounted to 15.9 per cent of net worth in 1983/4. Given that a return of 12 per cent on net worth is the normal allowance made for regulated industries, this suggests that additional revenue worth Rs 433 needed to be generated in 1983/4, requiring a price increase of 20.7 per cent.[a]

In January 1984, average coal prices were increased from Rs 145 to Rs 183 per tonne, an increase of over 26 per cent, bringing the coal industry, at least temporarily, into a reasonable profit bracket. In this situation, there appears little justification for adjusting coal costs faced by cement producers in 1984/5 on subsidy considerations.

Power

The magnitude of the power problem was indicated in Chapter 2. Power cuts and voltage fluctuations impose an extraordinary burden on a continuous process industry. It is for this reason that the industry is advised to make internal provisions for 40 per cent of its power requirements. These, however, impose additional burdens in terms of requirements of imported petroleum and the need to transport coal on an overstretched rail network.

Power shortages in the country are attributed very largely to the inefficiency of the State Electricity Board (SEBs) and to the subsidization of power tariffs, which fail to allow adequately for the investment component. An illustration of the SEBs' inefficiency is the fact that in the early 1980s the power generation, transmission and distribution system in Uttar Pradesh was paying out as emoluments 180 per cent of value added.[b] On the investment com-

---

[a] Based on finances of coal companies presented in Public Enterprises Survey, 1983/4.
[b] EDA, 1984.

ponent, another study has found that prices based on generation-distribution costs alone provide an implicit subsidy of 9 to 42 paise per unit depending on the assumptions. If capital recovery occurs in ten years at 12 per cent interest, the subsidy element is 22 paise per kwh.[a] Given the average price of around 65 paise per kwh in 1984/5, this suggests a subsidy of 33 per cent on the capital account alone. To account for the SEBs' losses as well, a price adjustment of 50 per cent for arriving at the resource cost of power appears reasonable.[b]

Transport

As indicated earlier, the failure of the railways to cope with the freight traffic available has led to a decline in the rail transport co-efficients for both coal (now around 65 per cent) and cement (at 50 per cent). Generally, rail transport is used for long distances while short hauls are dispatched by road. In this context although it would be incorrect to say that there is an overall shortage of transport facilities in the country, the full commitment of the rail network certainly suggests that some adjustment in rail transport prices is required. An adjustment of 20 per cent should provide a reasonable approximation of the resource cost of rail transport.

Manpower costs

As indicated earlier in this chapter, minimum wages in MCPs are just one-third those paid by the large sector in response to unionization and the Cement Wage Board awards. It is evident from the order of magnitude of MCP wages that they pay the opportunity cost of labour whereas the large sector pays a substantial premium. On account of the shortage of skilled workers and managerial staff in India it is likely that these are paid their opportunity cost by both sectors. On the basis of a significantly higher ratio of skilled : unskilled workers in the large sector than in MCPs, a reduction of around 50 per cent in the large sector manpower costs is required to obtain an approximation to opportunity costs of manpower in MCPs.

Taxes

Three types of taxes are realized from the cement industry. These are mineral royalties collected by state governments on the mining

[a]Vyasulu and Krishnan, 1986.
[b]This will also account for the additional burden on foreign exchange and transport imposed by captive generation.

of limestone, coal and other raw materials, central excise (Rs 205 per tonne in 1984/5) and state sales taxes (6 to 8 per cent of the ex-factory price). The latter two contribute about 20 to 25 per cent of the ex-factory price of non-levy cement. Mineral royalties in the range Rs 5-9 per tonne of limestone may be regarded as the economic value imputable to exhaustible resources. The economic cost of services such as roads which are not collected by other means, however, requires the levy of 'corrective taxes'. At 1984/5 prices the level of such taxes cannot be more than Rs 50 per tonne (compared to the Rs 280 actually collected as excise and sales taxes).

Table 5.6 incorporates the calculation of resource cost on the basis of the adjustments discussed above. For the purpose of this calculation the cost of cement at the point of retail sale rather than ex-

Table 5.6. Economic valuation of cement (1984/5 prices) (Rs/t of cement)

Conversion factors:	Coal	1.00	
	Power	1.50	
	Labour (large-scale)	0.50	
	Transport	1.20	
	Taxes	+ Rs 50 per tonne	
		NCB (MPL)	*Large scale*
Production cost[1]		567.27	545.67
Transport of cement[1]		30.00	115.58
Total		597.27	661.25
Cost adjustment:			
Power		76.03	60.00[2]
Labour		-	(−)22.52
Transport—coal		15.96	10.80
—cement		-	11.56[3]
Taxes		50.00	50.00
Net increase		141.99	109.84
Annual capital cost[4]		117.76	149.47
Total economic cost		857.02	920.56

Source:
[1] At market prices from Table 5.3.
[2] Estimated.
[3] Based on transport of an average of 50 per cent of output by rail.
[4] As for Table 5.3, 13 per cent interest.

factory has been considered because significant resources are expended in transporting cement after production—particularly from large plants. On this basis, the resource cost of cement produced by a 100 tonnes per day MCP amounts to Rs 860 and that by a large plant to Rs 920 per tonne. The difference of Rs 60 per tonne is attributable entirely to the transport of cement over long distances. Indeed, this transport cost even neutralizes some of the economical features of the large plant such as its better use of power and fuel. Thus in terms of resource cost, MCPs do appear to enjoy a slight advantage over large plants, albeit only in the context of the distorted market organization brought about by the freight equalization policy. In the near future, the abolition of freight equalization could lead to a rationalization in the markets served by large plants and a reduction in the average distance to the product market. This is likely to reduce the resource cost advantage of MCPs to insignificant levels.

For the purpose of assessing economic efficiency of production, the resource cost in Table 5.6 for the large scale sector has to be compared on an ex-factory basis[a] with the landed cost of imported cement. The ex-factory cost of Rs 793 per tonne is substantially higher than the average c.i.f. (cost, insurance, freight) price of Rs 585 per tonne in 1984. The domestic resource cost coefficient (DRC) of cement production is thus 1.36, suggesting the relative inefficiency of the Indian cement industry today.[b]

However, despite the prescriptions of neoclassical trade theory this cannot become a reason for abandoning cement production altogether because:

- the export prices of cement f.o.b (free on board) from Europe appear to be lower today than in 1979. These low prices ($20-22 per tonne in 1985) are related to a glut in world markets which is leading many Southern European and Arab producers to dump cement at marginal prices. It is a situation which, by its very nature, is bound to change, albeit over a number of years.
- in a country of continental dimensions with an abundance of all the major raw materials, an efficient cement machinery manufacturing capability and a shortage of foreign exchange[c] it would be

[a] Net of transport cost.
[b] This compares with the landed cost of Rs 479 per tonne in 1979 and a resource cost of Rs 355 per tonne. The DRC then was in the relatively efficient region of 0.75.
[c] Imports exceeded exports by over 80 per cent by value in 1985/6 and by 44 per cent in 1984/5.

difficult to justify abandoning cement production altogether. In viewing this in terms of a foreign exchange constraint, the need for a shadow exchange rate, which would (perhaps) reduce the domestic resource cost to less than one, is implicitly recognized.

CHAPTER 6

The Reality of Mini-cement

The apparent contradiction of the laws of economics implied by the competitiveness of MCPs can be explained in terms of differential resource utilization by the VSK MCPs compared to rotary kiln large scale plants. The reality of mini-cement as it emerges from the discussion in the foregoing chapters is best considered within the framework set out in Chapter 4.

An assessment

Raw materials and the utilization of small deposits
Large volumes of raw material necessitate relatively large labour forces at the quarry site in labour intensive Indian conditions resulting in managerial difficulties including lack of selectivity in mining. The smaller volumes necessary for MCPs require smaller labour forces and thus make it easier to manage and maintain quality. The need to go further and further from the factory for quality limestone has a significant effect on transport costs. Despite diseconomies of transporting small volumes, MCPs are not at a significant disadvantage due to the relative proximity of the quarry face.

Large-scale rotary kiln plants and most VSK MCPs (which are based on the intergrinding of coal and other raw materials early in the process) have to ensure homogeneity of feedstock either by highly selective mining or by creating separate dumps of various grades of limestone. The intermixing process used for the ATDA VSK, on the other hand, is ideally suited to variable quality raw materials, as feedstock composition is only finalized at the homogenization stage just prior to feeding into the kiln. Using this process, it thus becomes

possible to utilize scattered deposits of calcareous materials, otherwise regarded as marginal, for cement production.[a]
     Despite the case of a few plants proposed or established in Uttar
Pradesh, Himachal Pradesh and the north-eastern states (particularly
in the hill districts of these areas) there is little evidence of a systematic
tendency for these plants to be established at locations with small
deposits. Most of those in Madhya Pradesh, Rajasthan and Karnataka are merely tapping parts of gigantic and well known belts
of limestone.

Reduced burden on the transport infrastructure
     The discussion in Chapter 5 shows that MCPs reduce the transport
burden in cost terms from 16 per cent of the selling price to around
10 per cent. In a country with an over-burdened transport infrastructure this has to be seen as a significant saving. In the Indian context, the difference is aggravated by the locational distortions caused
by the freight equalization policy. As a result, large plants have,
historically, been sited close to raw material sources without regard
to markets.
     There is little difference between MCPs, although those located
closer to steel plants will impose an even lower burden on account
of the proximity of fuel supply. This is only likely to apply to a few
plants located in Madhya Pradesh, Orissa and Andhra Pradesh in
the near future.

Reduced packing and distribution costs
     There is little from the experience of the MCPs covered in the
course of this study to suggest that packing costs are reduced to any
significant extent. Though some 'gate sales' do take place, this is
virtually always in the conventional packing—jute bags. In fact, local
excise authorities do not facilitate the sale of unpacked cement. Per-
mission to sell in the unpacked form is usually withheld because of
the relative difficulty this creates for the authorities in keeping a check
on the quantity sold.
     Though MCPs were found to be using a mix of new and old bags,
this does not represent any significant advantage as large sector units
are also reported to be following this practice.

---

[a]However, this advantage is limited by the fact that only one of the MCPs in operation in India is based on this principle owing to the late finalization of the design.
Efforts at commercial diffusion of the design are now being made.

Other than ex-factory retail, sales are through local dealers, so distribution costs are not significantly affected either (except in the case of the transport component discussed earlier).

Possibility of producing other than OPC and utilizing waste materials
All MCP techniques available claim to be appropriate for OPC production. As far as is known, none of the MCP units produces anything other than OPC and/or PPC.

In contrast to the other techniques, the ATDA plant has been designed specifically to utilize marl and (if possible) kankar. Other than a casual use of marl for producing good quality lime, these are largely waste materials. A TC of 65 to 85 per cent for marl means that the material is of marginal quality for cement production. While ATDA has demonstrated the technical feasibility of using this material for cement production with a VSK, technical opinion suggests that the real advantage of the ATDA technique is not in utilizing marginal material but rather in facilitating the use of *variable quality* materials.[a] While marl deposits may, on balance, be more variable in quality than limestone deposits, there is some suggestion that poor (and careless) mining in India often results in highly variable quality limestone reaching the factory stockyard. In coping with this problem the ATDA technique appears to be superior to other MCP designs.

Capital investment and employment
The lower unit capital investment entailed in VSK MCPs is evident from the figures in Tables 5.1 and 5.3 with Rs 1,050 per installed annual tonne for the large sector comparing with Rs 761 for NCB (100) and Rs 900 for Saboo (20). These costs are set in context by the findings of a World Bank study which showed that the Indian cement machinery industry was highly efficient, with a DRC of around 0.4. The difference in unit cost is, thus, related to basic characteristics of the different types of technology employed. Within each type, significant scale economies exist with the minimum economic scale for VSK being 100 tonnes per day and for rotary kiln, around 2,000 tonnes per day.

[a]A plant manufacturing OPC from marginal 'lime-kankar' and based on the rotary kiln technology was established at Charkhi-Dadri in Haryana as long ago as 1938. This is a large plant with a 750 tpd kiln.

A 25 per cent import content for modern rotary kiln plants compared to negligible imports for VSK plant fabrication, further tilts the balance in favour of the latter in the context of an overvalued exchange rate.[a]

Far higher employment per unit of investment in MCPs is also clear from the table below:

	Fixed capital (Rs lakhs)	No of workers	Capital/worker (Rs lakhs)
Saboo (20)	59	80	0.74
NCB (100)	251	120	2.09
Large scale	7600	1000	7.60

According to the Seventh Plan Working Group Report, total capacity expected to be created during the Seventh and Eighth Plan periods (up to 1995) is 37 m tonnes. The capital and employment implications of this if capacity is created in the large versus the mini sector, are compared in Table 6.1.

Table 6.1. Capital and employment implications of investment in cement capacity

	Saboo (20 tpd)	NCB (100 tpd)	Large-scale (2,250 tpd)[1]
Capacity (m tonnes)	37	37	37
No of plants	6,167	1,122	50
Capital investment[2]			
Fixed	3,663	2,816	3,800
Working	429[3]	401[3]	335[4]
Total	4,092	3,217	4,135
Employment ('000)	493	132	51[5]

Source:
[1] Assumed average size of 0.75 m tpa for new plants.
[2] Rs crores
[3] Estimates based on discussions with plant managements.
[4] Based on WGR, 1984 estimates of Rs 5.0 crores for 0.5 m tonnes p a and Rs 7.8 crores for 1.0 m tonnes tpa.
[5] WGR, 1984 estimates.

[a] WGR, 1984. This import content is expected to decline to 10 per cent over the next few years.

Over 6,000 plants (of the Saboo type) would be required to produce an additional 37 m tonnes by 1995. This appears to be a
phenomenal figure, except when compared with the 4,800 MCPs in
China in 1983. Using the NCB/MPL technique the number of MCPs
would be reduced to 1,100 whereas only 50 large sector plants would
be required.

Concentration on the Saboo technique would keep the overall
capital required at around the level of the large sector. The
NCB/MPL design would cut it down to just 78 per cent.

It is in terms of employment generation that the Saboo plant per-
forms best. Direct employment created by Saboo type plants would
be of the order of 500,000 persons as well as seasonal employment
for another 100-150,000 persons in quarrying. The NCB/MPL
design, by contrast, would create direct employment for just 130,000
persons whereas modern large scale units would benefit only 50,000
persons directly.

Lower gestation period

Delivery periods of MCP plant and machinery are in the range
of 8 to 12 months. This suggests a gestation period in the range 12
to 18 months for such plants. By contrast, the gestation period for
large plants lies in the range two to five years. Most plants take three
to four years to establish.

Dispersal of production

It is clear from Table 6.1 that the Saboo technique is the most
appropriate of the three in the matter of dispersal of production.
To the extent that there are at least a few small deposits of cement
grade limestone in virtually every state in the country, concentration of MCPs can result in very considerable dispersal of production. However, it should also be recognized that a large proportion
of the production would still have to come from the limestone rich
states of Andhra Pradesh, Karnataka, Madhya Pradesh and Gujarat.
To the extent that production is dispersed, local product availability would reduce the transport burden and increase accountability
on the part of producers.

Investment by persons of limited means

The relatively low capital costs of MCPs naturally make this investment and production opportunity available to entrepreneurs of
more limited means than the large-scale plant. However, the need

for a minimum of Rs 12 lakhs as margin money (on working and fixed capital) even for investment in a Saboo plant, as well as the institutional awareness/influence necessary to obtain loans of the order of Rs 50 lakhs, renders the technology inaccessible to even those who might be classified as the rural rich. The threshold of acceptability for investment in MCPs lies at the level of dominant entrepreneurs or traders in the smaller district towns (or large market towns in the larger districts). Cooperatives (of the quasi-public sector type) can also be regarded as feasible investors at this level.

Managerial issues and skills for fabrication and operation

Discussion with machinery manufacturers reveals that skills in fabrication are certainly simpler for MCPs. In the case of operational skills, the relationship is more complex. There is a spectrum of techniques available ranging from the basic Saboo plant to the 100 tonnes per day NCB/MPL plant with sophisticated instrumentation and quality control systems. At the former end of the spectrum the plant is easy to fabricate (at large workshops), has a relatively small number (and value) of bought-in motors and components from large industry and is easy to maintain (needing the skills of no more than good heavy vehicle mechanics). At the latter end, the number of bought-in components increases and the sophistication of the workshop requires more skills. Maintenance, in this situation, involves larger inventories of gear boxes and components for replacement rather than 'on-the-spot' repair.

Conversely, however, plant operation reduces somewhat in skills and degree of supervision required with a shift to the more sophisticated end of the spectrum. Rougher equipment and instrumentation in the Saboo techniques necessitates more careful handling of materials and operation of the kiln than in the NCB/MPL design.

While the ATDA technique simplifies materials handling, when raw material quality varies it still requires careful supervision to ensure product quality.

Ultimately, however, it should be emphasized that both the nature of the VSK technology and the nature of market competition from large plants is such for MCPs that they are really suitable only for operation by entrepreneur-managers. Careful resource management, close supervision of production and aggressive marketing, particularly in the initial stages, are crucial to the success of each venture.

Deficiencies in maintenance leading to high repair costs of machinery, waste of production owing to faulty instrumentation and high administrative costs are commonly reported from large-scale plants. Major teething troubles from modern 1.0 m tonnes p.a. plants have also been reported. These deficiencies, as well as many of those discussed earlier in this section, stem from technological and human shortcomings which are an inherent feature of India's level of economic development. In a more developed economy, energy consumption would be lower, coal and limestone would be better mined and graded at the pithead or quarry site, and better skilled as well as more committed labour and management would stem other production deficiencies in the large sector. By contrast, the tight proprietorial control and lower overall skill requirements of much of the mini-cement sector enables the VSK technology to realize its potential within the limitations of the country's economic environment.

Energy

Though energy efficiency is not part of the stated rationale for mini-cement plants, a consideration is essential on account of the importance of the issue for the chronically energy-constrained Indian economy. Whereas energy consumption in Indian VSKs lies in the range 1,000-1,100 kcal of heat per kg of clinker, consumption in the more efficient rotary kilns is around 900 kcal per kg. Similarly, whereas power consumption in MCPs exceeds 120 units per tonne of cement, in efficient large plants consumption lies in the range 100-110 units per tonne.

It is worth noting, however, that poor quality coal with low heating value (3,500-4,500 kcal per kg compared to a norm of 5,000 kcal per kg) and high ash content (30 to 35 per cent compared to a desirable maximum of 20 to 25 per cent) also increases costs by increasing quantity requirements, by necessitating higher maintenance costs and on account of the need to use limestone with a higher lime content. VSKs use coke breeze (a by-product of blast furnaces) and are not so severely affected by these problems.

Environmental issues

The nature of the problem at limestone quarries is such that neither MCPs nor the large-scale sector can be absolved of responsibility for environmental depredation. The established and planned units in the hill areas consist of both small rotary kiln and VSK plants;

neither can be described as inherently less destructive in obtaining its raw materials. As implied earlier, similar devastation may be the result of the industry's operation elsewhere; it is only the relative economic insignificance and sparse population of most limestone belts that protects the industry from further scrutiny.

While research results related to dust emissions from VSKs are not available, casual observation is sufficient to assert that their performance is not significantly better than large-scale plants. To the extent, however, that the semi-wet process employed by VSKs reduces overall emission levels below those of dry process plants, the former do enjoy some advantage over the most modern large-scale technologies in use in India. However, the remote location of most large plants mitigates this effect. MCPs generally located closer to markets may, in fact, cause greater overall pollution from their emissions.

Cement for the rural messes

Throughout the years of acute cement shortage its effects were more pronounced in the rural than in the urban areas. In the marketing and distribution of a scarce bulk commodity the relative ease and magnitude of sales in concentrated urban markets far outweighs the temptation of higher unit prices that could be obtained from a dispersed rural one. To the extent that price control and freight equalization are effective, the incentive to sell in urban markets is even greater. In the matter of state supply, the working group report laments that the state governments are experiencing major difficulties in the matter of distribution of cement to rural areas.[a] The alleviation of the ensuing difficulties for rural consumers is another important argument advanced for the dispersal of production through MCPs.

In referring to the difficulties of rural consumers, however, it is usually assumed that it is the large proportion of rural poor who are denied access to the material. Given the information in Table 3.9 this would suggest that those denied access would use alternative cementitious materials. In order to determine the extent to which rural consumers face difficulty in obtaining cement, the effect this has on the economic profile of the consumer and, in consequence, the extent to which MCPs could be instrumental in serving the needs

[a]WGR, 1984, para, 11.5.

of the rural poor, a survey of cement consumption was undertaken in the vicinity of the ATDA pilot plant at Mohanlalganj. The survey incorporated a listing of all the houses in 15 villages to determine the type of construction and identify structures constructed anew, wholly or partly, during the preceding three years. A sample survey of households owning new constructions was then undertaken to determine the magnitude of the problem of access and the economic profile of cement consumers.

Table 6.2 shows that of the 1,017 houses in the 15 villages, just 10 per cent were found to be pukka while 80 per cent were semi-pukka.[a] Less than 22 per cent of households had undertaken construction over the past three years. The type of new construction undertaken suggests a distinct shift to the building of pukka structures. Only 37 per cent of new construction were wholly kuchcha. Table 6.3 presents the distribution of cement consumption by per

Table 6.2. Distribution of houses in the surveyed villages by type of construction

Type of construction	No of houses	%	New construction	%
Pukka	104	10.2	44	19
Semi-pukka	282	27.7	96	43
Kuchcha	631	62.1	83	37
Total	1017	100.0	223	100

Table 6.3. Distribution of cement consumption in rural Lucknow

Income group (Rs per capita)	Total no of houses	% of total	Sampled houses	Cement users	Bags used	% of total
⩽ 600	200	19.7	9	3	31	3.5
600 – 1,100	405	39.8	33	10	74	8.4
1,110 – 2,000	258	25.4	26	13	149	16.8
> 2000	154	15.1	35	31	632	71.3
	1017	100.0	103	57	886	100.0

[a]Pukka means hard, literally and is used to refer to constructions which use non-erodable processed or unprocessed mineral materials for construction. Semi-pukka is a construction which is partly pukka. The third alternative, kuchcha, means made from erodable or biodegradable materials.

capita income group. In the Table those with per capita incomes of less than Rs 1,100 can be described as poor.[a] As the Table shows, 57 of the 103 sampled newly constructed houses had used some cement for construction. The distribution of consumption, however, was highly skewed. The consumption figures in Table 6.3 have been plotted as a Lorenz curve in Figure 6.1. This shows that whereas the poor 60 per cent of the population in rural Lucknow consumed just 12 per cent of the cement in the three years preceding January 1985, the richest 10 per cent consumed as much as 64 per cent of all the cement used. This illustrates the extent to which rural cement consumption is dominated by the wealthy.

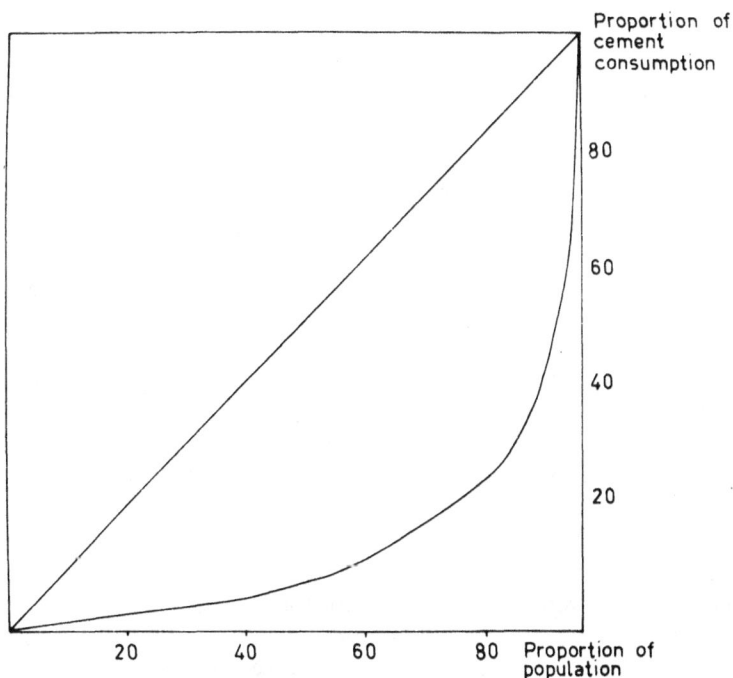

Figure 6.1   Lorenz distribution of cement consumption in rural Lucknow

[a] This is an updating of the officially defined poverty line of Rs. 3,500 per annum for a family of five at 1978/9 prices. At current prices this translates to Rs 5,500 per annum, when inflated by the consumer price index for agricultural labour.

The beginning of the reference period of the survey coincided roughly with the introduction of dual pricing in February 1982. As a result of the ready availability of free sale cement through as many as eight retail outlets within a 20 km radius of the Mohanlalganj plant, none of the households surveyed reported any difficulty in obtaining access to cement. Only one of the new structures had utilized an alternative surkhi lime mortar for construction. All the others were either mud, mud mortar or cement mortar constructions. Given the roughly similar cost of alternative materials, this leads to the conclusion that cost rather than physical access is the crucial factor in the skewed rural consumption of cement. Further, local transport costs from the distribution outlet of just Rs 0.50 to 1.80 per 50 kg bag suggests that it is the selling price rather than this cost which is relevant.[a]

As the discussion in Chapter 5 showed, at market prices the difference between MCP costs of production including transport to the retailer (in Uttar Pradesh conditions) and average production and transport cost for the large-scale sector is no more than 13 per cent. The difference of Rs 95 obtained (at 1984/5 prices) when translated to a proportion of selling price amounts to no more than 7.5 per cent. In an industry with extremely high cost variations between plant locations, this difference cannot be regarded as significant. It is clear that MCPs cannot make cement available to consumers at a significantly lower price than large plants. On the basis of the survey of consumption in rural Lucknow, it follows that the mere presence of an MCP in the vicinity is of little benefit to the low income consumer.

Finally, the importance of cement as an input into the creation of an economic and social infrastructure which benefits the rural poor is manifest. However, the importance of MCPs for this purpose is not. Virtually all infrastructure (apart from factories) is created by government agencies which acquire cement supplies at levy prices through the regulatory mechanism. By contrast, MCPs are not obliged to supply cement at levy prices and consequently they make no direct contribution to infrastructure. With an increasing supply of cement (in recent years) and the absorptive capacity of government agencies restricted by budgetary considerations, the

[a] Physical access may not be a problem in Mohanlalganj due to the proximity of the city of Lucknow. Elsewhere it may be a more important constraint but is likely to be associated with an even more skewed consumption pattern.

government has progressively been reducing the levy obligations of large-scale plants. In this situation of easy cement availability, production by MCPs of the order of 2.5 per cent is a relatively unimportant contribution to overall availability. Even if all the proposed MCP capacity materializes by the end of the Seventh Plan period, MCPs will make only a small contribution (11 per cent) to overall availability. The importance of the mini plant for the low income consumer is, therefore, extremely limited.

CHAPTER 7

Conclusions: Small versus Large in the Indian Cement Industry

This study set out to investigate the relevance of the VSK mini-cement technology to the Indian economic situation. The detailed description and discussion of developments in the cement industry as a whole established the background of strict (and unremunerative) price control and consequent shortages against which the adaptation to Indian conditions and diffusion of MCP technology in India became a reality.

For the future, cement demand is expected to grow rapidly at a rate of 10 per cent p.a. With the control regime accounting for decreasing proportions of large-sector production, investment in the industry has gathered momentum and the trend of rapid expansion is expected to continue well into the Eighth Plan period.

At the time of writing (late 1986), the cement industry is showing signs of alarm (at least in its public statements) at an emerging 'surplus' in the market which has resulted in stagnation in the free market price of non-levy cement over the past three to four years.[a] This alarm, however, is likely to be exaggerated by:

- the desire to obtain a reduction in the levy obligations of large-scale plants and an increase in retention prices.[b]
- increased proportions of output entering the non-levy free market, increasing stocks and depressing prices in the short run.
- the balancing of the supply-demand equation and the disappearance of the suppliers' market for the first time.

[a]Except for a short period in the second half of 1985.
[b]Some 'relief' (to use the industry's terminology) was obtained when the government announced a 6.5 per cent (Rs 24.50) increase in the retention price of levy cement on 15 December, 1986. Simultaneously, the levy cement quota for large-scale plants was reduced by 10 to 50 per cent for old units and 30 per cent for new and 'sick' units.

A two-way adjustment of expectations—producers to a more competitive market and consumers to an easy supply situation—is likely to occur in response to this situation. Freed from the constraining effect of shortage (only now properly eliminated), demand is expected to grow more naturally after a short adjustment period. In the medium to long term (up to 20 years) therefore, demand is unlikely to be a constraint on the growth of the cement industry in general and the MCPs in particular.[a]

With regard to pricing policy also, there is little cause for alarm in the long term. While the trend to liberalization could well lead to the abolition of price control altogether, this is unlikely to cause a collapse in the free market price. Levy cement is currently used almost exclusively for infrastructure projects sponsored by the government. Consumption of this type is almost entirely price inelastic so that demand is unlikely to suffer any significant fall if and when price control is abolished.

In the matter of cement price trends and their implications for the economy as a whole, however, it is difficult to be sanguine. These are determined not only by the supply-demand equation (which largely affects the margin available to producers) but also by the production costs of the leading suppliers (ACC, the Birla Group and CCI). Unit production costs incurred by the large sector in India are significantly higher than those in developed countries—Rs 550 per tonne compared to around US$ 25 or Rs 300 per tonne in Europe in 1985. These high production costs are related to a number of factors:

- high raw material costs apparently resulting from inefficiencies at the mining stage and from high transport costs
- high energy consumption—around 900 kcal of heat per kg of clinker in India compared to just 750 kcal of heat per kg of clinker in the developed countries and power consumption of around 110 units per tonne of cement in India compared to just 90 units per tonne elsewhere
- managerial deficiencies resulting in high repair costs of machinery, waste of production due to faulty instrumentation and high administrative costs. Major teething troubles from modern 1.0 m tonnes p.a. plants have also been reported.

---

[a]Short-term difficulties resulting from downturns in the economy as a whole, cannot, of course, be ruled out.

Over a period of time, some improvements in specific energy consumption can be expected from the conversion of the remaining 33 per cent of capacity from wet process to dry process. Growing experience with plant operation and increased competitiveness in the industry is also likely to lead to improvements in management. The accentuating power shortage coupled with the inefficiency of the SEBs, on the other hand, will continue to necessitate high cost internal power generation as well as higher than necessary payments for grid power. Similarly, the inefficiency of the coal mining companies and the poor quality of Indian coal will keep coal costs at a high level.[a] Thus, while cement production may be marginally resource efficient (in economic terms), prices of cement are likely to continue to be high in comparison with the international market.

In relation to mini-cement plants, the major finding of this study is that under Indian conditions the VSK MCP represents a viable alternative to the large-scale plant under appropriate technical and institutional conditions. The differences between the two types of plant are related to the basic characteristics of the technologies employed and their interaction with the Indian development situation. These are summarized in Table 7.1 and outlined below.

Resource sustainability

The resource cost of cement produced in a 100 tonnes per day VSK is no higher than that produced in a relatively efficient large rotary kiln. As MCPs currently do not enjoy any special policy concession other than complete freedom from price control, this finding is independent of policy changes.

In the utilization of capital, material and transport resources MCPs enjoy a clear advantage over the large sector but a significant disadvantage in their utilization of energy resources. While better resource utilization enhances the sustainability of MCP production, energy inefficiency is a major disadvantage in a country where good quality coal is in short supply and power shortages are a chronic problem. Overall, therefore, there is little difference in resource sustainability between the two sectors.

Environmental factors

In the quarrying of limestone for cement production, neither MCPs nor the large sector can be absolved of responsibility for

---

[a]Even if coal is beneficiated at washeries, this process will in itself increase costs.

Table 7.1. Comparative resource utilization in MCPs and large scale plants

Resource	MCP	Large scale
Capital	Cost 27% lower per annual tonne of capacity created,	Cost 27% higher per tonne of cement produced when annualized over the life of the project
	Import content—negligible	Import content—25%.
Raw material	Small volumes more easily managed with labour intensive quarrying	Large volumes: difficult to manage labour force and maintain selectivity at mining stage
	Quarry face relatively near factory	Quarry face may recede considerably from factory leading to increased transport cost
	Flexibility of intermixing process allows use of variable quality raw materials	Variable raw materials have to be batch graded before use
Energy	High consumption: 1,000-1,100 kcal heat/kg clinker	900 kcal/kg clinker (cf 750 kcal/kg in developed countries)
	120 kWh per tonne of cement	100-110 kWh/tonne (cf 90 kWh/tonne)
Labour	Cost: low Skills: basic, technical	Cost: high Skills: advanced engineering.
	Output: 200 tpa per employee	Output: 600 tpa per employee
Transport - materials - cement	High, especially coke breeze Low	High but less than MCP High
Management	Proprietorial, exercising tight control but subject to inefficiency through inexperience	Hired—poor maintenance, high repair costs, high administrative costs

environmental depredation. It is simply the relative economic insignificance and sparse population of most limestone belts that protects the industry from closer scrutiny.

Though the level of atmospheric emissions from cement plants far exceeds the limits specified in pollution control standards, the relatively benign nature of lime means that the overall effect is more of an inconvenience than an ecological hazard. Here again there is little to choose between MCPs and large plants.

Indigenous capabilities

The negligible import content of MCP machinery compared to the 25 per cent imports necessary for modern large-scale cement plants not only saves valuable foreign exchange reserves, it also implies that the capability to manufacture the former type of machinery is fully indigenous. Coupled with the better local availability of skills for, and higher labour content of MCP operation, this suggests a greater sustainability of VSK technology diffusion. In managerial terms also, VSK has an advantage in that the necessary commitment required for efficient production of quality output is more likely to be provided by the proprietorial control typical of MCPs than by the hired managements of the large scale sector. These factors are inherent to the technology-development interface at India's level of economic development. At the same time, the growth of the MCP sector helps to disperse production facilities and contributes to the spread of an industrial culture in the country.

In development terms, however, one major factor has to be set against these advantages. Under present conditions the VSK is essentially a static technology. Its use is on the decline internationally (including in China) and an atmosphere of doubt about its capabilities exists in India. Consequently, little active research is being undertaken to improve its energy or economic efficiency.[a] Large-scale rotary kiln production, on the other hand, is undergoing constant R&D, with expanding frontiers and growing technical sophistication.

For a country like India, with a broad-based and growing technical capability, investment in large-scale cement technology represents

---

[a] With the possible exception of a private machinery manufacturer in India whose capabilities in this respect can best be described as limited within the frontiers of the technology. Having introduced VSK operation in India, the NCB has tended to rest on its laurels.

an investment in technology assimilation and skills development as well as in efficient production of an essential material. The indigenous capability and dispersion effects of MCPs cannot, therefore, become a prescription for abandoning large-scale cement production altogether.

Conclusion

The consideration of VSK cement production as an appropriate technology for Indian conditions is undoubtedly constrained by the requirement that all cement produced and sold in the country should conform to the fairly stringent standards of Portland cement. The experience of VSK operation has conclusively shown that MCPs cannot supply Portland cement at prices significantly below prevailing market prices determined by the large cement companies. Their present effect on overall availability is also restricted, though in limited areas of chronic shortage (such as the northeastern states) they can have a significant effect on both availability and price.[a] VSK cement production in India, therefore, neither facilitates the use of cement as a final consumption material by the poor nor does it make any special contribution to the development of infrastructural facilities which contribute to economic progress. Indeed, given that controlled price cement is supplied by the large sector only, it is the latter which makes this important contribution to development.

Similarly, the savings implications of dispersed production are limited by the existence of centripetal links between the typical MCP investor—the large town trader/manufacturer—and the large cities. Rural investment by such persons is limited by the lack of sufficient perceived production opportunities. Direct or indirect, the benefits of the technology for the rural poor are not likely to be very significant.

Balancing the resource efficiency of MCPs against energy inefficiency, indigenous sustainability and industrial dispersion against technical stagnation and, environmentally, locational convenience against (some) atmospheric and visual pollution, no definite conclusion in their favour emerges. In the short to medium term, MCPs will undoubtedly have a positive developmental effect. However, if

---

[a] In other countries, where lower cement standards are acceptable for certain applications, the relative flexibility of MCP operation could make cheaper cementitious materials available.

the technical stagnation of VSKs continues, the large-scale plant will inevitably emerge as more appropriate in the long run. In this perspective, the place of mini-cement in the Indian economy is essentially as a capital-saving technology for the intermediate entrepreneurs. For the time being a parallel development of both sectors is the most sensible policy prescription. The reality of the VSK technology in Indian conditions constitutes only a weak justification for the rationale.

Appendix Tables

Table 1. Cement dispatches under various priority categories (m tonnes)

Year	RC		ORC		Public sale		Total	
1970	4.42		0.81		8.34		13.57	
		(32.6)		(6.0)		(61.5)		(100.0)
1972	5.23		1.38		8.81		15.41	
		(33.9)		(8.9)		(57.2)		(100.0)
1974	6.57		2.24		4.98		13.79	
		(47.6)		(16.2)		(36.1)		(100.0)
1976	6.28		1.15		10.36		17.79	
		(35.3)		(6.5)		(58.2)		(100.0)
1978	9.23		2.28		8.88		20.39	
		(45.3)		(11.2)		(43.6)		(100.0)
1980	9.24		3.68		6.51		19.44	
		(47.5)		(19.0)		(33.5)		(100.0)
1982	9.67		4.14		2.58		16.39	
		(59.0)		(25.3)		(15.8)		(100.0)
1984	11.16		2.53		2.53		16.22	
		(68.8)		(15.6)		(15.6)		(100.0)

Source: CCO, various

　　　　　　　　　MINI-CEMENT

Table 2. Availability of limestone (m tonnes)

State	Limestone reserves	Number of plants Large[1]	Number of plants Mini[2]	Leased deposits	Available deposits	Available deposits as a percentage of total reserves
North						
Haryana	19.30	2	-	15.70	3.60	19
Himachal Pradesh	1,504.10	8	-	220.00	1,284.10	85
Jammu & Kashmir	207.30	1	-	92.90	114.40	55
Rajasthan	2,904.33	8	3	750.85	2,153.48	74
Uttar Pradesh	894.50	2	2	216.20	678.30	76
	5,529.53	21	5	1,295.65	4,233.98	77
South						
Andaman & Nicobar	9.10	-	-	-	9.10	100
Andhra Pradesh	19,831.90	19	12	953.56	18,878.34	95
Karnataka	11,233.74	8	7	1,405.50	9,828.24	88
Kerala	24.50	1	-	24.60	-	0
Tamil Nadu	472.00	7	-	333.70	138.30	29
	31,571.34	35	19	2,717.36	28,853.98	91
East						
Arunachal Pradesh	317.50	-	-	91.10	226.40	71
Assam	185.10	1	1	42.20	142.90	77
Bihar	799.15	6	2	392.01	407.14	51
Manipur	12.20	-	1	2.00	10.20	84
Meghalaya	2,542.70	1	-	40.00	2,502.70	98
Nagaland	377.00	-	1	2.00	375.00	99
Orissa	362.02	1	-	75.09	286.93	79
West Bengal	7.40	-	-	-	7.40	100
	4,603.07	9	5	644.40	3,958.67	86
West						
Diu	45.00	-	-	-	45.00	100
Gujarat	10,184.00	5	4	225.00	9,959.00	98
Madhya Pradesh	6,901.23	10	3	692.08	6,209.15	90
Maharashtra	848.30	3	3	232.80	615.50	73
	17,978.53	18	10	1,149.88	16,828.65	94
Total India	59,682.47	83	39	5,807.29	53,875.18	90

Source: CRI, 1984

[1]Capacity range 2-10 tonnes per annum

[2]Capacity 0.66 tonnes per annum.

Table 3. Coat reserves in India (m tonnes)

State/union territory	Reserves of coal	Percentage of total
STATES		
Andhra Pradesh	5,515	5.3
Assam	245	0.2
Bihar	35,259	23.7
Gujarat	180	0.2
Haryana	-	-
Himachal Pradesh	-	-
Jammu & Kashmir	53	0.05
Karnataka	-	-
Kerala	-	-
Madhya Pradesh	17,219	16.4
Maharashtra	6,699	6.4
Manipur	-	-
Meghalaya	395	0.4
Nagaland	-	-
Orissa	10,233	9.8
Punjab	-	-
Rajasthan	-	-
Sikkim	-	-
Tamil Nadu	2,032	1.9
Tripura	-	-
Uttar Pradesh	-	-
West Bengal	26,253	25.1
UNION TERRITORIES		
Andaman & Nicobar	-	-
Arunachal Pradesh	610	0.6
Chandigarh	-	-
	104.693	100.0

Source: WGR, 1984.

Table 4. Power requirement, supply and shortages[1]

Year	Anticipated requirement	Supply	Shortage	Percentage shortage
1974/75	77,600	66,647	10,953	14.1
1975/76	83,508	74,909	8,599	10.3
1976/77	88,489	83,365	5,124	5.8
1977/78	102,180	86,343	15,837	15.5
1978/79	108,535	97,349	11,186	10.3
1979/80	118,370	99,302	19,068	16.1
1980/81	120,118	104,932	15,186	12.6
1981/82	129,245	115,274	13,971	10.8
1982/83[2]	136,849	124,225	12,624	9.2

Source: Ahluwalia, 1984
[1] As per cent of energy delivered at station bus bar
[2] April 1982 to January 1983

Table 5. Effects of conversion of wet to semi-dry/dry process

Item	Process			
	Wet	Semi-dry	Dry	
			with only SP	with SP & precalcinater
Heat consumption (kcal/kg clinker)	1,300-1,600	900-1,100	800-950	750-850
Power consumption (kWh/t of cement)	110-115	115-120	120-125	120-125
Kiln output for given size (percent)	100	130-150	130-150	250-300
Investment cost per tonne of annual capacity for conversion (Rs)	-	550-950	950-1,050	1,150-1,250

Source: WGR, 1984
Note: The above are average ranges. Extreme values could in exceptional cases be somewhat lower than the lower limits or substantially higher than the upper limits.

Table 6. Retention prices and additional charges allowed to cement producers
(Rs per tonne)

Date	Retention price[1]		Packing charges	Excise duty	Freight charges[2]	FOR price	
1965/6	83.75		na	na	na	159.00	
1970/1	103.86		30.84	31.92	30.47	197.09	
1971/2	105.37		35.05	32.84	31.46	204.72	
1972/3	105.09		39.02	34.75	33.91	212.77	
1973/4	116.20		33.52	37.75	34.80	222.27	
1974/5	161.40		43.60	66.82	41.11	312.93	
1975/6	160.07		40.98	81.24	50.93	333.22	
1976/7	158.55		40.94	82.00	56.10	337.59	
1977/8	176.26	296.00[3]	41.65	65.00	55.39	338.30	458.04
1978/9	236.06	296.00	47.27	68.25	57.20	408.78	468.72
1979/80	258.85	296.00	63.16	68.25	60.09	450.35	487.50
1980/1	252.66	309.65	62.30	71.50	66.28	453.66	509.73
1981/2	324.63	344.39	63.74	71.50	76.22	535.72	555.85
1982/3	352.00	704.75[4]	76.48	135.00	88.00	653.61	1004.23
1983/4	348.00	734.00	89.93	205.00	144.00	771.77	1172.93
1984/5	377.14	734.00	132.62	205.00	144.00	858.76	1215.62
1985/6	388.00	841.63	139.37	225.00	144.00	896.37	1350.00[5]

Sources: CCO, 1982; Cement Manufacturers' Association.
[1] Retention price here is FOR price minus excise duty and freight and packing charges.
[2] Average freight paid by cement producers up to 1970, freight allowed by Cement Controller's Office.
[3] Price allowed to new units.
[4] Non-levy realization.
[5] Estimated.

Table 7. Excise collections from the cement industry

Year	Rate (Rs per tonne)	Revenue (Rs lakh)	% of total excise revenue
1965/6	28.32	3,073	3.4
1966/7	28.32	3,217	3.1
1967/8	28.32	3,213	2.8
1968/9	28.32	3,496	2.6
1969/70	30.68	4,257	2.8
1970/1	31.45	4,407	2.4
1971/2	32.64	4,874	2.3
1972/3	34.75	5,489	2.3
1973/4	36.96	5,319	2.0
1974/5	58.99	8,056	2.4
1975/6	79.60	12,747	3.2
1976/7	79.16	14,220	3.3
1977/8	65.27	12,181	2.7
1978/9	68.25	13,440	2.4
1979/80	68.25	12,379	2.0
1980/1	70.80	13,673	2.1
1981/2	76.79	16,959	2.2
1982/3	140.83	33,626	4.2
1983/4	205.00	55,976	5.5
1984/5	225.00	63,170[1]	5.7
1985/6	225.00	69,650[2]	5.8

Sources: RBI, various; NCAER, 1978.
[1] Revised estiamte.
[2] Budget estimate.

Table 8. Profitability ratios

Year	Gross π as % of sales		Gross π as % capital employed		Net π as % net worth	
	Cement	All industries	Cement	Industry (all)	Cement	Industry (all)
1960/1	12.8	10.6	7.9	10.0	7.8	11.0
1965/6	15.5	10.7	11.0	10.1	11.2	8.9
1970/1	12.9	10.3	9.7	10.4	11.8	11.2
1971/2	12.3	10.0	9.5	10.4	9.4	10.5
1972/3	8.0	9.5	6.3	10.0	4.7	10.3
1973/4	3.7	10.5	2.8	11.0	−2.3	11.9
1974/5	3.5	11.4	3.2	12.8	−2.3	13.7
1975/6	6.8	10.2	8.9	11.3	12.9	9.9
1976/7	6.6	10.0	7.3	11.6	4.9	9.8
1977/8	9.3	9.7	10.9	11.3	9.3	9.7
1978/9	8.8	9.5	9.6	11.7	10.4	11.5
1979/80	8.0	10.1	8.3	12.6	7.6	14.5
1980/1	1.8	10.5	1.7	12.3	4.5	14.4
1981/2	5.0	10.2	4.5	11.8	6.6	14.5
1982/3	15.6	9.5	14.1	10.3	33.9	12.9
1983/4	12.9	8.6	12.2	8.9	23.4	18.4
1984/5	9.1	8.9	7.9	9.3	8.9	9.1

Source: RBI, various.

Table 9. Inter-regional average freight, 1984 (Rs per tonne)

From/to	North	South	East	West	Total	Quantity (m tonnes)	% of total
North	105.15	-	98.48	88.72	96.09	4.48	27.7
South	430.02	62.52	267.95	129.44	100.45	4.07	25.2
East	-	61.93	69.05	-	69.04	3.09	19.1
West	162.18	133.1	203.9	74.87	124.75	4.54	28.1
Total	133.74	66.65	137.46	90.58	106.24	16.17	100.0

Source: CCO, 1984.

Table 10. Average freight paid for levy cement (1984)

Region	State	Av. freight (Rs/t)	Freight/ FOR price (%)[1]	% difference
North	Chandigarh	106.02	12.3	-
	Delhi	166.57	19.3	+ 7.0
	Haryana	123.71	14.3	+ 2.0
	Himachal Pradesh	72.40	8.4	− 3.9
	Jammu and Kashmir	205.86	23.8	+ 11.5
	Punjab	186.81	21.6	9.3
	Rajasthan	78.29	9.1	− 3.2
	Uttar Pradesh	111.76	12.9	+ 0.6
	Total region	133.74	15.5	+ 3.2
East	Arunachal Pradesh	178.52	20.7	+ 8.4
	Assam	222.42	25.7	+ 13.4
	Bihar	92.56	10.7	− 1.6
	Manipur	127.18	14.7	+ 2.4
	Meghalaya	31.95	3.7	− 8.6
	Mizoram	160.32	18.5	+ 6.2
	Nagaland	130.30	15.1	+ 2.8
	Orissa	149.04	17.2	+ 4.9
	Sikkim	145.89	16.9	+ 4.6
	Tripura	210.56	24.4	+ 12.1
	West Bengal	147.58	17.1	+ 4.8
	Total region	137.46	15.9	+ 3.6
West	Dadar/Nagar Haveli	109.50	12.7	+ 0.4
	Goa, Daman & Diu	111.67	12.9	+ 0.6
	Gujarat	68.77	8.0	− 4.3
	Madhya Pradesh	56.47	6.5	− 5.8
	Maharashtra	121.88	14.1	+ 1.8
	Total region	90.58	10.5	− 1.8
South	Andaman & Nicobar	305.64	35.4	+ 23.1
	Andhra Pradesh	68.08	7.9	− 4.4
	Karnataka	76.20	8.8	− 3.5
	Kerala	70.58	8.2	− 4.1
	Lakshadweep	-	-	-
	Pondicherry	61.52	7.1	− 5.2
	Tamil Nadu	49.47	5.7	− 6.6
	Total region	66.65	7.7	− 4.6
	All India	106.24	12.3	

Source: CCO, 1984.
[1] Rs 864.65 per tonne.

Table 11a. Raw material and fuel requirement/tonne of cement

Raw material	Cost Rs/tonne	Requirement/t cement ATDA	NCB	Saboo	Cost/t cement (Rs) ATDA	NCB	Saboo
Marl	40	1.48	-	-	59.20	-	-
Limestone	50	-	1.20	1.19	-	60.00	59.50
Kankar	40	0.08	-	-	3.20	-	-
Clay	15	-	0.21	0.22	-	3.15	3.30
Laterite	320	-	-	0.01	-	-	3.20
Blue dust	320	0.04	-	-	12.80	-	-
Total							
Raw meal		1.60	1.41	1.42	75.20	63.15	66.00
Gypsum	280	0.06	0.04	0.05	16.80	11.20	14.00
					92.00	74.35	80.00
Coal							
Steam coal	800	0.05	-	-	40.00	-	-
SLV coal	700	0.10	-	-	70.00	-	-
Coke breeze	720	0.10	0.21	0.20	72.00	151.20	144.00
					182.00	151.20	144.00
Power (kWh)	-	150	125	90	179.22	152.05	117.00

Table 11b. Manpower requirements

Type	Number Saboo	ATDA	NCB	Average emoluments	Total cost p.a. (Rs lakhs) Saboo	ATDA	NCB
Administrative	7	9	9	1,200	1.01	1.30	1.30
Technical							
Plant	14	6	9	750	1.26	0.54	0.82
Laboratory	5	8	5	800	0.48	0.77	0.48
Production							
Semi-skilled	20	20	60	500	1.20	1.20	3.60
Unskilled	22	35	35	350	0.92	1.47	1.47
Total	80	78	118		4.87	5.28	7.67
Cost per tonne (Rs)					81.17	70.40	25.82

Table 11c. Other production costs

Item	Estimated cost/year ('000 Rs)			Cost/t (Rs)		
	ATDA	NCB	Saboo	ATDA	NCB	Saboo
Office overheads	90.0	356.4	72.0	12.00	12.00	12.00
Packing material	750.0	2970.0	600.0	100.00	100.00	100.00
Lubricants	50.7				6.76	
Repairs, maintenance and consumables	225.0	1336.6[1]	210.0[1]	30.00	45.00[2]	35.00
Insurance[3]	70.6	203.4	43.4	9.41	6.85	7.23
	1186.3	4866.3	925.4	158.17	163.85	154.23

Source: .

[1] Includes cost of lubricants.

[2] Assuming 33 per cent fixed costs on the presently reported cost of Rs. 75.62.

[3] 1 per cent on machinery, 0.5 per cent on building.

Bibliography

Ahluwalia, I J, 1985, *Industrial Growth in India—Stagnation Since the Mid-Sixties.*

Business India, various issues.

CCO, Various, *Cement Production and Despatches,* New Delhi: Office of the Cement Controller of India.

Cement, various issues. (Journal of the Cement Manufacturers' Association)

CIAR, 1983, *Cement Industry Annual Review 1983.*

CMA, 1964, *The Cement Industry in India 1914-1964,* New Delhi: Cement Manufacturers' Association.

CMA, 1984, *Analysis of Cost of Cement Production and Price Realisation* 1984, New Delhi: Cement Manufacturers' Association.

CRI, 1983, *Techno-Economic Viability of Mini Cement Plants,* New Delhi: Cement Research Institute of India.

CRI, 1984, 'Status of Limestone Availability and Potential Sites for Major Cement Plants', *Cement,* April-June.

DGM, 1981, *Progress Report on the Detailed Investigations of Marl and Kankar Deposits in District Lucknow, Barabanki and Rae Bareilly,* Agarwal, A K, Rizvi, M H Singh, R M, Uttar Pradesh, Lucknow: Directorate of Geology and Mining, June.

EDA, 1984, The Industrialisation of Uttar Pradesh: A Position Paper, Lucknow: Economic Development Associates (*mimeo*)

EPW, 1985, 'Economic Efficiency of Machinery Sector in India: Findings of a World Bank Study' *Economic and Political Weekly,* October 12.

Economic Survey, Various, Ministry of Finance, Government of India.

Economic Times, Various.

Financial Express, Various

Garg & Bruce, 1980, *Mini Cement—Project Proposal and Feasibility Report,* Lucknow: Appropriate Technology Development Association.

Hajra, S, 1983 *Economics of Scale in Cement Industry,* New Delhi: Economic and Scientific Research Foundation.

Iyenger, M S, 1975, 'On an Alternative Approach,' *Science Today,* January 1975.

Li et al, 1984, *Mini Cement Workshop—Cement Industry in China,* 1984, China: China Cement Development Centre.

NCAER, 1978, *A Study of Price Control and Impact of Excise Duty on Selected Industries,* New Delhi: National Council of Applied Economic Research.

NCAER, 1979, *Cement Industry in India—Problems and Prospects,* New Delhi: National Council of Applied Economic Research.

NCAER, 1980, *International Market Survey of Cement,* New Delhi: National Council of Applied Economic Research.

RBI, various, *Report on Currency and Finance, Volume I and II,* Reserve Bank of India.

RBI, 1983, *Monthly Bulletin,* Reserve Bank of India, July.

Reporter: B N, 1984, 'Case for Bulk Cement Distribution'. *Financial Express,* October 4, 1984.

Spence, R J S, 1979, *Appropriate Technologies for Small-Scale Production of Cement and Cementitious Materials.* ITIS. Rugby.

Stewart, D F, 1985 'Options for Cement Production in Paupa New Guinea: A Study in Choice of Technology' *World Development,* Vol 13 No 5.

TECS, 1984, *Analysis of Costs of Production of Large Scale Units in the Indian Cement Industry,* Tata Economic Consultancy Services, Bombay.

Vyasulu V and Krishnan Uma R. 1986, 'Electricity Price: What the Investment Component Is' *Economic Times,* 9 June.

WGR, 1984, *Report of the Working Group on Cement Industry Seventh Plan 1985-90,* Government of India.

World Bank, 1980, India: Cement Subsector study, Washington D C (*mimeo*)